AMERICAN PRISONS
A CRITICAL PRIMER ON CULTURE AND CONVERSION TO ISLAM

By

SpearIt

American Prisons, A Critical Primer on Culture and Conversion to Islam
Copyright ©2017 SpearIt

ISBN 978-1506-904-87-0 PRINT
ISBN 978-1506-904-88-7 EBOOK

LCCN 2017951100

August 2017

Published and Distributed by
First Edition Design Publishing, Inc.
P.O. Box 20217, Sarasota, FL 34276-3217
www.firsteditiondesignpublishing.com

Library of Congress Cataloging-in-Publication Data
SpearIt
American Prisons, A Critical Primer on Culture and Conversion to Islam
/ written by SpearIt.
    p. cm.
    ISBN 978-1506-904-87-0 pbk, 978-1506-904-88-7 digital

1. SOCIAL SCIENCE / Islamic Studies. 2. / Criminology. 3. /Prison Culture. 4./Sociology.

A51213

DOI 10.21899/978-1506904870

Table of Contents

Introduction

This book is for readers who seek to gain a critical understanding of prisons in contemporary America, especially those interested in the intersection of race and Islam. The work consists of published research and writings, articles, book chapters, and other scholarly works, which span over a decade of investigation. Compiled into an easy to read format, this book is organized along four major themes, each of which has several dedicated chapters. The works have been edited from the original for content and flow, and all citations have been removed for brevity's sake. For readers desiring access to citations in their entirety, the Appendix has links to the original works that contain all citations.

This catalogue of writings will be of great resource for many. At its baseline, the work will be a must-have for students of prison, religion, law, anthropology, sociology, and criminal justice among other fields of study. This book, however, will be of interest far beyond academic circles, and should reach the masses, as well as political and institutional decision makers. As Michelle Alexander's The New Jim Crow has popularized the plight of prisoners and sparked the country's interest in the racial injustices that surround systems of mass incarceration, this book takes readers inside the walls to examine the most salient problems behind bars.

Prison culture and life behind bars capture the American imagination, perhaps like no other subject. From documentaries, TV series, films, video games, and cartoons to rap songs, even the newest Minions movie, Americans remain fascinated with the problems and consequences of imprisoning other humans. This book offers a voyeuristic window into this "other" world to consider the forces that shape life behind bars. More specifically, the story of the black prisoner turned Muslim in prison is a large part of the script as Black Americana, and it occupies a large part of this imagination.

This book, to be sure, is also intended for those interested in ways to change the status quo. Not only is it a road map of some of the most pressing problems in law and society, but also prescriptions for reducing pain and suffering behind bars and beyond. Hence the book should also be of value for lawyers, activists, policymakers, and institutional actors interested in social justice and criminal justice reform.

The chapters that follow draw on a range of data. Sources include interviews and written correspondence with current and ex-prisoners, documentary research, congressional hearings, and I draw on my own personal and practical experiences. I have taught for the Prison University Project at California's death-row facility, San Quentin State Prison, as well as taught Corrections Law in law school, in addition to serving on the Advisory Board of the Prison Program at Saint Louis University—a unique program that offers courses to both inmates and staff. I have also been active in the American Bar Association's Corrections Committee and its work to restore Pell Grant Funding for prisoners. Collectively, these sources and experiences make this book an authoritative and critical statement on the state of punishment in America.

Part I

The Origins of Criminal Justice and Religion in Prison

There is a long and notable history between prisons and religion. Gods have been born and died as prisoners; holy families have been imprisoned; Abrahamic traditions have founded prisons, which in turn, have served as spaces for prisoners to "find" God. The very notion of bondage underlies practically all theological and even non-theological traditions that stress "liberation," "freedom," and "salvation" as core tenets.

The following chapters offer a theoretical map for considering the complexities of modern imprisonment and religion. The first begins by presenting a historical frame for understanding criminal justice systems as a historical foil for cosmic struggles between the forces of good and evil. The next chapter narrows the focus to the role of religion in the modern American prison context, paying close attention to the role of Islam for African-American inmates. The final chapter in this cluster employs ritual theory to fathom why there are so many ethnic minorities in prison. It theorizes the turn to mass incarceration as a type of civil sacrifice that makes Black and Brown bodies the scapegoats of a great civil ritual. Together, these chapters illustrate the complex, multi-layered nature of prisons and religion, and they provide a backdrop for considering prison culture for the rest of this book.

Chapter 1

Criminal Justice & Religion

The world's great religious traditions have held in common the need to deal with what we today call "crime" or "criminals." As history has shown, when an individual strays from the community norm, religion typically offers punishment as remedy for the problem. From the *Laws of Manu* in orthodox Hinduism, which outlines the proper punishment to be meted out to the different classes of criminals, to the Hebrew Bible's "spare the rod, spoil the child" statements, religious communities often engage with the problem of deviancy and, more specifically, how to punish it. In today's era of secular nation-states, the state is now largely responsible for the task of punishing offenders of the law—even though the state law, in some cases, might be an extension of religious law.

In the United States, one can see an infusion of religious ideas in the punishments of the state. And although the notion of "separation of church and state" is held in high esteem, in practice, history shows that Christian ideals can be linked to the entire U.S. legal system. The criminal justice system is no exception, and the impact of religion is apparent from the very beginning of its development. In turn, the criminal justice system has played an influential role in the history and day-to-day realities of religious practitioners and their com-munities. As home to the largest prison population in the world, well over two million and counting, the U.S. criminal justice system is a key factor in the religious practice of many.

CRIMINALS AND ALTARS

> For eighteenth- and nineteenth-century Christian society the prisoner was the scapegoat. To pay for their sins prisoners needed to be expelled, transported, locked out of sight behind walls, prevented from human contact, hanged.
>
> —Timothy Gorringe from
> *God's Just Vengeance*

From the Hindu god Krishna, who was born in prison, to Jesus of Nazareth, who was incarcerated and executed by Roman officials, the connections between criminality and religiosity are profound. In many ancient societies, religion and law were synonymous. Religion was the guidance that told people how to act properly and how to punish one who strays. In a climate where monotheism, polytheism, and paganism competed, breaking the law was, in essence, sinning against God or the divinity of the gods. Throughout history, political systems such as oligarchies, democracies, and dictatorships have moved away from an explicitly religious substrate. Often deeming themselves "secular," in reality, they are deeply indebted to religious thought, symbols, and practices.

In the United States, the notion of "civil religion" has been used to describe the way in which U.S. nationalism fuses with Christian piety. In this theocratic-democratic overlap, the state and religion meld together into an official guise, into the machine by which rituals and religion find expression. At the very extreme, this view might correlate Abraham to George Washington, the Bible to the Declaration of Independence and Constitution, and the gospel to democracy.

In the U.S. secular state, one is no longer in God's country as a matter of law, and there are no more sinners as far as the state is concerned. Instead, there are criminals, and they are individually responsible for repaying what they have taken from society by their criminal conviction. And there is no doubt that many in the United States believe that God has a special relationship with America, which is perhaps best revealed by the phrase "God Bless America." But even from the earliest times of the colonies that were to become the United States, the notion of "providentialism" or "manifest destiny" provided a theological basis to justify the expansion of colonial settlements.

At the juncture of religion and criminal justice are a number of theoretical questions. One is how to conceive of the influence of religion in legal punishment, including how the inner mechanics of religious violence work. Or what legitimates the use of violence?

BLACK HISTORY:
THE DYNAMIC INTERPLAY OF RELIGION AND CRIME

We're bringin' 'em to a Christian land. It's got to be better for them than that heathen Allah they got with them now.
— From the television series
Roots

Ever since the passing of the Thirteenth Amendment to the U.S. Constitution (1865), criminal justice has been constitutionally linked to the question of slavery. According to the language of section I of the

Thirteenth Amendment, "Neither slavery nor involuntary servitude, except as a punishment for crime where of the party shall have been duly convicted, shall exist within the United States." Rather than completely abolish slavery, the amendment made slavery legal for those convicted as criminals; rather than wiping out the institution, this piece of legislation merely reclassified who could be enslaved. From 1865 to the present, this amendment has been the legal link between chattel slavery and the type of slavery seen today in U.S. prisons.

This connection also indicates chattel slavery as the early ancestor of the U.S. criminal justice system. Without doubt, 250 years of slavery had made Americans quite proficient in the tactics of bondage and punishment. Even prior to chattel slavery evolving into its modern forms, there were deep connections between the institution of slavery and religion. For some, Christianity was used as a justification for the enslavement of black Africans; if a slave owner bothered to share his faith with slaves, it usually focused on the story of Ham and the curse that befalls his people (and all blacks as a consequence)— to be indentured to whites. For many who owned slaves, such interpretations of the Christian faith legitimized the slaves' cursed condition. Thus, whether done in sincerity or in guise, religion was used in defense of slavery.

During the slave trade, over 50,000 trips were made within the triangular passage, from Europe to Africa to the Americas, and back to Europe again. Among the millions of captured slaves who survived the passage from Africa to the West (the middle passage) were among the very first Muslims to arrive during the colonial era—early movements that have been well documented. The slave trade was thus not merely a matter of whites enslaving blacks, but significantly, of Christians enslaving Muslims, and at the very beginning of U.S. history, slavery and religion were intertwined in complex ways. This is especially true when considering that Christian groups were a major force in the abolition of chattel slavery.

By the time of eighteenth-century America, a group of Christian fundamentalists, known as the Quakers, were instrumental in developing what became the modern penitentiary, an institutional innovation that was deeply rooted in the ideology of rehabilitation. Although "an eye for an eye" logic and public shaming were the order of the day, the Quakers had a mind for helping criminals, through compassion. This rehabilitative model based itself on the religious notion of "penitence," the need to reconcile one's misdeeds with the will of God. To these penal reformers, a crime against society was a sin, a correlation that birthed the need for religious repent—hence the original and lasting designation "penitentiary," or the place of penitence. Modern prisons are greatly indebted to these Quaker-influenced experiments that were designed to resurrect criminals and release them back to society, healed and ready to become productive members.

Although many are unaware of the religious history of U.S. prisons, religion plays a major role in day-to-day operations of the institution and lives of the inmates. Moreover, behind bars, religious conversion is alive and thriving. In prison folklore, the "born again" Christian has been a staple, both in popular discourse and in the prison environment, for decades. Muslim conversions are nothing new either; Malcolm X converted to Islam in prison half a century ago, and he was far from the first. More recently, in testimony to the Senate Committee of the Judiciary, *Terrorist Recruitment and Infiltration in the United States: Prisons and Military as an Operational Base*, one scholar described as follows the power and appeal of Islam in prison:

> Currently, there are approximately 350,000 Muslims in Federal, state and local prisons—with 30,000-40,000 being added to that number each year . . . These inmates mostly came into prison as non-Muslims. But, it so happens that once inside the prison a majority turns to Islam for the fulfillment of spiritual needs. . . It is estimated that of those who seek faith while imprisoned, about 80% come to Islam. This fact alone is a major contributor to the phenomenal growth of Islam in the U.S.

For others, however, the practice of religion in prison may be for less devout reasons—or even something of a con game, a temporary or transitory appropriation—and used for protection, perks, or simply to get out of the cell or to socialize. Sincere converts and practitioners have been distinguished primarily according to whether they continue practicing after release—some abandon religion; others keep the faith.

As the prior sections have attempted to demonstrate, there is a perpetual struggle between the forces of religion and crime. For prisoners, religion can be a force for rehabilitation or even resistance. Embedded in this struggle is the fact that a state's "criminal" can simultaneously function as a religion's "messiah." The examples in history are numerous; likewise, the branding of "criminal" by the state serves to enhance the drama of the religious narrative, where ultimately the Divine gets the last laugh. Whether it be Jesus resurrecting from capital crucifixion or Malcolm X resurrecting from a life of crime, the state is represented as nothing more than an instrument that is used to carry out a greater destiny. Religion needs the state, because the state represents the most awesome power that humans have configured; it is this very power, the power of the state—even at its climax of power—that is ineffective and impotent against the power of God.

Chapter 2

Religion in Prisons

THE RELIGIOUS ROOTS OF INCARCERATION

Religion in prison is a complex topic. Although theoretically the prison's own origins are deeply indebted to religious ideology, practically, today's prisons are centers of conversion where inmates develop their relationship with God. Although religion in prison generally has a positive influence on inmates, including helping to reduce drug addiction and recidivism, sometimes religion can lead to extreme outcomes, especially when followers interpret a religion as authorizing violence. Sometimes prison policies and conditions help to stoke the flames of discontent. What follows offers an assessment of religion in prisons, which also considers ways that prison can minimize their role as a contributor to these and other problems.

Although the word "religion" technically refers to the Abrahamic traditions, in prison it may refer to an array of practices, beliefs, or philosophies, including those of Buddhism, Hinduism, and Native American traditions. For some inmates, religious narrative speaks directly to their incarceration, including narratives like the Exodus from Egypt and the incarceration and capital execution of Jesus by the Roman state. These stories hold meaning for Christians and Muslims, who make up the majority of religious inmates; both find meaning in Jesus' imprisonment, torture, and killing, and Muslims identify their imprisonment with the persecution of the household of the prophet Muhammad. Hence not only is there cosmic significance in imprisonment, but its modern iteration is the creation of religious thought.

FREE EXERCISE BEHIND BARS

Courts have interpreted the term "religion" and the scope of rights afforded to practice religion in prison. The definition of religion is critical since whether an inmate is afforded religious rights depends first on whether the inmate adheres to a religion. For inmates deemed to be following a legitimate religion, religious freedom is limited compared to life on the outside. In prison, the practice of religion is often restricted in some way, and more so for some groups than others. In American prisons, Muslims, for example, have claimed to suffer ongoing oppression, which has driven many inmates to seek justice in the courts. Muslims in prison have had an important role in both the struggle for prisoners' rights and the struggle for their souls.

Defining Religion & Constitutional Rights in Prison

The First Amendment to the U.S. Constitution enshrines the right to practice one's religion. According to the language of the amendment: "Congress shall make no law respecting an establishment of religion, or prohibiting the free exercise thereof..." The first part of the amendment is commonly called the Establishment Clause, and has come to be understood as the foundation for the separation of church and state. The next part, commonly called the Free Exercise Clause, requires the government to refrain from interfering with people's religion and their right to practice freely. Inmates typically make claims on Free Exercise grounds.

To determine whether a state's action infringes upon a prisoner's right to practice religion, a court must first decide what qualifies as a religion or religious activity for First Amendment purposes. Yet what constitutes a "religion" for inmate purposes is no easy task, especially since the U.S. Constitution never provided a legal definition for the term. However, history shows that in the quest to define religion, courts have moved from a very Christian-centered concept to a much more expansive view of what constitutes a religion.

By today's legal standards, a religion need not espouse a supreme being or the existence of God to fall within the scope of the First Amendment's protections. However, this has not always been the case as exemplified in early rulings like *Davis v. Beason* (133 U.S. 333 (1890)), where the Supreme Court adopted a monotheistic worldview in an early attempt at definition: "The term 'religion' has reference to one's views of his relations to his Creator, and to the obligations they impose of reverence for his being and character and of obedience to his will." In subsequent cases, the Court would add contours to this understanding, including unabashed statements like "we are a religious people" and that "this is a Christian nation," and one justice characterizing the essence of religion as "belief in a relation to God involving duties superior to those arising from any other human relation" (*Church of the Holy Trinity v. United States*, 143 U.S. 457, 471(1892)).

Breaking from this earlier line of cases, the Supreme Court went on to develop a more functional understanding of religion, including those sincere beliefs held by individuals which parallel the role of God in other peoples' lives. The more traditional, theistic concept was first challenged by the Second Circuit ruling in *U.S. v. Kauten* (133 F.2d 703 (2d Cir.1943)), in which Justice Learned Hand announced a broader concept of religion when interpreting the phrase "religious training and belief" as found in the Selective Service Act of 1940: "Religious belief arises from a sense of the inadequacy of reason as a means of relating to the individual to his fellowmen and to this universe...which categorically requires the believer to disregard elementary self-interest and to accept martyrdom in preference to transgressing its tenants."

In the modern context, courts have developed a broader understanding of religion. In *Torcaso v. Watkins* (367 U.S. 488 (1961)), the Court invalidated a provision that required all public officials in Maryland to profess a belief in God. The Court held the provision as unconstitutional since it imposed a burden on non-believers whose religion did not endorse the concept of God. The Court supported its rationale by noting the shades of religious pluralism in the country: "Among religions in this country which do not teach what would generally be considered a belief in the existence of God are Buddhism, Taoism, Ethical Culture, Secular Humanism and others."

In *Africa v. Pennsylvania* (662 F.2d 1025 (1981)), a federal appellate court refined the meaning of religion beyond its Christian baseline. In this case the court recognized the inherent difficulties of deriving a viable definition: "Few tasks that confront a court require more circumspection than that of determining whether a particular set of ideas constitutes a religion within the meaning of the First Amendment." Noting that the Supreme Court had "never announced a comprehensive definition of religion," the court nonetheless noted that religion can be understood as concerned with "fundamental and ultimate questions." Although the beliefs may be of a theistic or non-theistic nature, to constitute a religion, they must be comprehensive and shared by members of the group. In its opinion, the Court cautioned against prison staff and their attitudes toward traditional religions and the branding of unfamiliar faiths as secular. Although it expanded the scope of what could qualify as a religion, the court ruled that Africa's MOVE organization was a secular philosophy as opposed to a religion, adding that members did not share a comparable belief system and lacked almost all formal characteristics seen in most recognized religions.

How case law defines "religion" is at the heart of an inmate's ability to raise claims for the right to exercise religion. When American prisoners challenge administrative policies or behavior they often bring two claims: one based on claims alleging violation of the Religious Land Use and Incarcerated Persons Act (RLUIPA) and one based on the Equal Protection Clause, alleging violation of First Amendment right to free exercise of religion. Even though the two claims are based on the same facts, courts apply a separate analysis to each.

Previously, Congress enacted the Religious Freedom Restoration Act of 1993 (RFRA) to address potential burdens on an inmate's right to free exercise of religion. This act changed the standard of judicial review to the higher "strict scrutiny" standard and prohibited the government from substantially burdening religious exercise without a compelling justification. Shortly after its enactment, however, the Supreme Court deemed the RFRA to be unconstitutional as applied to state and county prisoners.

In response to this ruling, Congress passed the Religious Land Use and Institutionalized Persons Act, 42 U.S.C.S. 2000cc (RLUIPA) in 2000. According to the statute, prison officials cannot impose a substantial burden on an inmate's free exercise of religion unless the burden supports a "compelling interest" of the facility and unless the facility uses the "least restrictive" means of furthering its interest. Today, the majority of claims are brought by state inmates under RLUIPA.

Although RLUIPA provides a statutory basis for claims to free exercise of religion, as previously mentioned, inmates may also sue on constitutional grounds. The prevailing standard in equal protection litigation traces back to a pair of 1987 Supreme Court decisions, *Turner v. Safley* and *O'Lone v. Estate of Shabazz*. The former case examined restrictions on an inmate's right to marry, establishing that "[w]hen a prison regulation impinges on inmates' constitutional rights, the regulation is valid if it is reasonably related to legitimate penological interests" (*Turner v. Safley*, 482 U.S. 78, 89 (1987)). One week after the U.S. Supreme Court decided *Safley*, it applied the *Safley* standard to a free-exercise claim in *O'Lone v. Estate of Shabazz* (482 U.S. 342 (1987)). The plaintiff-inmates in this case challenged prison policies preventing Muslims from attending Friday prayer services. The Court ruled that the policies were legitimate since they did not deprive followers of "all" forms of religious exercise. Although many acknowledge *Shabazz* was an important defeat for Muslims, it is also represented a victory of sorts since it helped cement the lasting mark Muslims have left on the current state of prisoners' right jurisprudence, which is examined next.

The Muslim Movement

The history of Muslim prisoners' rights begins after the 1950s, since prior to that "courts rarely intervened on behalf of prisoners on free exercise grounds. Previously courts took the attitude that their place was only to decide who was deserving of punishment, and not to direct the manner in which the punishment was meted out. In American prisons, Muslims were often denied equal opportunity to practice their religion. But by the early 1960s, places like California, although encouraging of inmates' participation in religious activities, did not extend the policy to Muslim prisoners. Some argue that prior to that time, Muslims were essentially approached in one of three ways: either the prison administration adopted a "hands off" doctrine, exercised "complete authoritarian" power, or simply displayed overt racism. In most situations, Muslims were typically without legal recourse.

This was true until a member of the Nation of Islam brought the first successful prison litigation that sought the right for Muslim inmates to practice their religion freely. Three years later in *Cooper v. Pate* (378 U.S. 546 (1964)), a Muslim inmate won a ruling that state prisoners have standing to sue in federal court under the Civil Rights Act of 1871. In *Northern v. Nelson* (315 F. Supp. 687 (N.D. Cal. 1970)), a California inmate sued the state to be allowed to receive copies of a Nation of Islam publication, *Muhammad Speaks*, and to compel facilities to make copies of the Quran available to inmates.

Since these early cases, Muslim prisoners have based claims on numerous grounds, albeit they have been largely unsuccessful. Inmates claim to have been denied *hallal* meats and other compliant foodstuffs, as well as prevented from performing *khutba* religious sermons during Friday prayer, participating in *jumuah* services, and reciting religious texts in Arabic. Muslims also claim to have been restricted to wearing beards no longer than one-quarter inch, or in some cases, at all, as well as prohibited from wearing *kufi* caps, traditional robing, or prayer beads. Other claims state Muslims have been required to choose between access to Islamic services or to the law library, denied access to an Islamic chaplain, and penalized for attending Muslim services. In some prisons, Sunni adherents claim they must pray with Shia or with members of the Nation of Islam. Shia adherents have sued for separate worship facilities, while others alleged being barred from holiday services while in disciplinary custody.

Prisoners litigate on other grounds as well. Allegations include being denied access to free Qurans or prohibited from the possession or use of prayer oils or other religious items, such as incense, leather socks, compass, hallal toothpaste, and prayer rugs. Inmates report being barred from celebrating Ramadan, *Eid ul Fitr*, or participating in Ramadan worship for breaking fast, and that officials have refused to acknowledge Shia holidays.

Other cases have contributed directly to shaping the lives of Muslims in prison. In *Fraise v. Terhune* (283 F.3d 506 (3d Cir. 2002)), a federal appellate court rejected a First Amendment claim by members of the Five Percent Nation of Islam, who had been labeled as a "security threat group" by prison officials. Although the members argued that their freedom to practice religion had been violated, prison officials testified that the Five Percent Nation was a violent youth gang that has incited gangs to violence and assaulted prison staff and other inmates. One official went on record stating that the group "constitutes one of the greatest threats to the social fabric of the prison." In *Mayweathers v. Terhune* (328 F.Supp.2d 1086 (E.D. Ca. 2004)), a U.S. district court ruled that a group of Muslim inmates who wanted to wear half-inch beards in accordance with their religious beliefs should be permitted to do so. Although the prison authorities voiced identification concerns, the court determined they were exaggerated since a half-inch beard did not pose the same identification problems as a long beard would, and since the beards were subject to daily inspections, much of the security concerns were eliminated.

As these legal struggles indicate, resistance by Muslims would help lay a foundation for Muslim inmates to become an organized and articulate group to emerge from the nascent prisoners' rights movement. Accordingly, Kathleen Moore has noted that Muslim groups often have been at the center of administrative and legal reform movements within state and federal penitentiaries. This trend continues in the present as Muslims are reported to have filed the majority of RLIUPA claims between 2001-2006, representing a total of 62 out of 229 cases (U.S. Commission on Civil Rights 2008).

CONVERSION: FROM CHRISTIAN TO ISLAMIC PENITENCE

In the prison context, "conversion" connotes at least two major demographic trends in American prisons over the last half century. On one hand is the conversion from a largely white inmate population to the current overflow of ethnic minorities; on the other is the turn from Christianity as the only religious option for inmates to becoming only one of many. In the prison's current spiritual setting, Islam garners the majority of religious converts.

But what exactly is meant by religious conversion? The word "conversion" derives from the Latin *con* + *vertere*, which refers to the act of "turning around" or "revolving." In *The Varieties of Religious Experience*, William James describes it as "a great oscillation in the emotional interest, and the hot places," often inspired by crisis, or suddenness. This observation linking crisis and conversion suggests that hardships may be antecedent factors for a turn in faith. Put plainly, the prison experience itself may help account for the prevalence of conversion in prison. This idea enjoys support in the present, as one researcher writes, "the first time a person enters [prison], he encounters an alien society over which he has almost no say. The message is 'do what you can to survive this experience.' There may be a feeling of shock or dread—or basic fear—that the newly admitted inmate feels upon finding himself facing a sentence of imprisonment." The privations of prison may also correspond to "dissonance the inmate feels about being in prison." In tune with James's early observations, one researcher notes that "potential converts are predisposed by psychological, economic, and social deficiencies and problems to seek membership in religious 'cults.' The nature of deprivation varies somewhat from one researcher to another, but the emphasis in any case is on the individual psychology, situation, and motivation for the potential convert."

Conversion is the transition from the old life to the new. Procedurally, conversion may unfold in three dialectical moments: "(1) turning away, (2) a state or period of suspension, and (3) a turning toward." It can represent a shift within the same religious structure, from no religious commitment to a devout religious life, or a shift from one religion to another. Religious conversions have been classified under two criteria: "First, depending on whether they emphasize more the process (evolution) or the instant (turning point) of conversion; second, depending on whether they focus more on the intellectual, emotional or pragmatic dimension of conversion." Conversion has been likened to "a process of identity change, potentially a total change of identity. It is a kind of rebirth. Conversion also changes the way one looks at the world...for it involves a radical break with the past." Conversion has also been characterized as a "grammar of dissent" that acts as a framework of resistance.

The American prison system is a major locus for religious conversion and practice. With well over two million people incarcerated, about one-third of inmates claim some form of religious affiliation. Other research shows that many had no strong religious preference before incarceration and it is estimated that among those who seek faith in U.S. prisons, some 80 percent turn to Islam, an aggregate the U.S.

Commission on Civil Rights (2008) estimates at nearly 10 percent of all American inmates.

Studies on religious conversion explore a number of issues specific to the prison setting. Topics include adjustment and coping, finding safety in prison, impacts on rehabilitation, and impacts on recidivism. Despite the relatively sparse research on this topic, scholars have provided several frameworks to consider: Islam in prison, reasons for conversion, the process of conversion, and the challenges of Muslims in corrections.

Why inmates convert in prison is a debated question. Some scholars propose that inmates convert as a distancing mechanism and way of expressing the erosion of one's social context, or that Islam has special appeal to those who are oppressed and unprivileged. Others relate conversion to adjustment to prison life such as resistance to the prison's unrelenting regimen or reaction to racism. Other research identifies five main reasons for conversion that include, personal crisis, protection, spirituality, outside influence, and to manipulate the prison system, while others credit interaction and association with Muslims as an important factor for conversion.

The process of converting is multifarious. Although some inmates may join Islam for immediate protection, genuine conversion is generally characterized as gradual and performed under little duress. For other converts, the process is seen as more of an intellectual endeavor that relates to a gradual turn toward the divine rather than religious experience. The timeframe for conversion is not easily known, and research often indicates the complexity of the issue, especially since some conversions appear to occur almost instantaneously, while others occur over a more gradual period.

Perhaps no prison-conversion story is better known than Malcolm X's. His autobiography outlines in striking detail how Islam transformed him from "Satan" to "Saved" to "Savior," a turn away from his old life and toward the Nation of Islam (NOI). For him, as with many others, the force of religion changed his perception of time and his predicament as a prisoner: "Months passed without my even thinking about being imprisoned. In fact, up to then, I never had been so truly free in my life."

Since Malcolm's times, the NOI has never lost focus of prison, and continues to view it as a central branch of ministry. Today, the NOI expresses concern for prisoners on its current official website posting of The Muslim Program's "What the Muslims Want." Article #5 states:

We want freedom for all Believers of Islam now held in federal prisons. We want freedom for all black men and women now under death sentence in innumerable prisons in the North as well as the South.

This stance, combined with many decades dedicated to prison ministry, is said to have given the NOI a formidable recruiting presence in the correctional setting.

Resurrecting Slaves of the State

At most large or "supermax" prisons, one will see the coming and going of priests, imams, and other clerical figures who contribute to the wide array of religious services held by members of Christian, Islamic, Jewish, Native American, and other faiths. Conversion in prison brings newcomers to the religious fold. As houses of penitence, penitentiaries have historically provided the space for spiritual transformation, producing the well-known "born again" Christian, but in present day, many believe they are a major recruiting ground for Islam. Some consider prisons to be "major centers of Muslim reflection and identity," and argue Muslim prison ministry is used "most effectively to penetrate nominal Christians..." The Encyclopedia of Prisons and Correctional Facilities notes that some 90% of 130 African-American masjids are actively involved in prison ministries and ministries to ex-offenders, and some provide temporary shelter for those released from prison.

In general, religion has positive effects on rehabilitating offenders. Research indicates that high levels of participation in religious activities can function as a viable correctional intervention to reduce juvenile delinquency, and in adult prisons, reduce prisoner misconduct. In a study on the attributes of those who escaped recidivism, religious transformation is one of the primary themes. The Department of Health and Human Services reports that the existing "body of literature is consistent with criminological theories supporting the claim that religious beliefs are inversely related to delinquency, crime and recidivism."

Islam's success in rehabilitation may relate structurally to the original intent of the penitentiary. The idea of Christian repentance resonates in Islam, or as D.C. Corrections Chaplain Imam Mikal Huda Ba'th explains, "[a] cursory review of the acknowledged intentions of Islam and the Quaker reformists shows that it is apparent the objective of both religious ideologies is to instill penitence in the criminal." Hence, the concept of prison is nothing new in Islam, and there are multiple references to imprisonment in the Quran. Robert Dannin has noted that "low recidivism rates and success in the rehabilitation of drug and alcohol addiction win tolerance, even approval, for Muslims." These indications support the Department of Health and Human Services' positive assessment of "how religious programming may be uniquely suited to both facilitate and augment the ongoing process of prisoner reentry."

Today, the impetus for conversion resembles what it was in the early days of American Islam, only some argue that today's harsh sentences and harsh prison conditions may provide even more compelling reasons. For inmates who convert to Islam, religion provides a narrative perfectly tailored to their current state of imprisonment, offering African-American Muslims a new hermeneutic of power: "historically captured, enslaved, and transported to the New World, then miseducated and forced to live an inferior existence...conversion to Islam adds new dimensions to that history, particularly as it emphasizes the presence of African Muslims and nonslave populations, evidence of resistance to Christianity."

Beginning with the enslavement and transportation of West African Muslims, contemporary Muslims cite the modern prison as the most current link in a chain of successive oppression of Muslims in America. Some believe converts are eager to adopt Islam in light of these historical markers, and to lay claim to Islam as an indigenous form of African and African-American religiosity. Identification of Islam with Africa is why many African-American prisoners call themselves "reverts"—to show they are returning to their original religion. As Dannin accords, "Islam teaches that those who lack the power to transform their material conditions need only reflect on the ideal Quranic past to see themselves as contemporary actors...Islam deals with social difference—even the distinction between freedom and incarceration—by collapsing the past, the present, and the future into a simultaneity of space and identity. To the extent that Islam succeeds in America's prisons, it offers a closed but definitive response to the modern dilemma of justice in an unjust world."

Chapter 3

Legal Punishment as Civil Ritual:
Making Cultural Sense of Harsh Punishment

It is customary for human beings to conventionalize and ritualize their necessities. Punishment becomes a social custom and is conventionalized and a ritual is set up for its elaboration.

—A. Warren Stearns from
The Evolution of Punishment

The Problem & Thesis

The central aim of this chapter is to examine the post-civil rights push toward harsh punishment through the cultural lens of ritual. The United States is one of the most punitive countries on the planet--the country is the world leader in imprisonment and is one of the top five that executes capital defendants. However, determining the catalysts of this turn to harsh punishment has proved vexing. Scholars have adequately explained *how* the end of the welfare state, followed by a proliferation of drug laws, police profiling, plea bargaining, and "tough on crime" law and policy were the major forces behind mass incarceration. This chapter's ritual framework helps explain *why*.

It argues that the spike in incarceration is a response to issues that have more to do with culture than crime; more particularly, with perceptions of danger, impurity, and superiority. This perspective itself is unoriginal, since sociologist Emile Durkheim long ago commented on punishment's social functions, which remains relevant to the present:

> In [h]is view, crime and its punishment are a basic part of the rituals that uphold any social structure. Suppose it is true that the process of punishing or reforming criminals is not very effective. The courts, the police, the parole system--none of these very effectively

> deter criminals from going on to a further life of crime. This would not surprise Durkheim very much . . . . [T]he social purpose of the punishment is not to have a real effect upon the criminal, but to enact a ritual for the benefit of society.

By challenging traditional dogmas, which view punishment as a rational and calculated response to crime, analysis of punishment through a ritual scope can add to the study of law. Sometimes changes that threaten the status quo, such as the passage of civil rights laws and controversial court decisions, produce social crises that lead to eras of harsh punishment, often disparately affecting "other" populations, mainly the poor and ethnic minorities. In these instances, punishment moves beyond the scope of its traditional justifications and becomes a tool for social control, which itself is a function of ritual activity. This chapter shows how the gains purported to have been won in civil rights struggles were forfeited to the criminal justice system in a dynamic interplay of ritual punishment, power, and social control.

The "civil ritual" thesis builds on two important themes. The first is "civil rights" since struggles over civil rights gave birth to the two distinct punishment trends discussed herein. The second theme is the concept "civil religion," which provides a framework for understanding ritual forms in public and political institutions. Together, these themes help to elucidate that "something" that drives Americans toward demanding harsh punishment.

This chapter theorizes punishment, but is not a theory of punishment. It is not about justifications of punishment grounded in legal or social norms. Rather, it is an attempt to articulate the core characteristic of punishment that gives rise to normative justifications. It does not address the classical questions that produce a cohesive punishment theory or attempt to ascertain proportionality, the scale of punishment, or the methods of execution. Rather than address the questions that create a general account of legal punishment, this chapter offers an interpretation of phenomena from a ritual perspective. This approach has largely escaped theoretical consideration by legal scholars, even though legal institutions charged with resolving conflict are entrenched in ritual activity. Its main contribution is to show how some of the harshness of punishment has to do with the strength of American religious and racial traditions.

Although arguing that legal punishment is a civil ritual may face resistance by legal academics on substantive grounds, it may also face opposition by some who think that open discussion of religion is in rather bad taste or represents "esoteric scholarship," legal nihilism, or reversion to mysticism. However, the ideas presented here lead to no such scheme. Instead, this analysis helps answer a more fundamental question--why punishment *in the first place?* Indeed, determining the first principles of punishment is difficult since they are so commonplace so as to be nearly invisible. This chapter's ritual emphasis, rather than leading legal scholarship astray, gets to the heart of why some must suffer so that others may feel secure.

Ritual Theory & Application to Crime

Broadly speaking, ritual activity might best be conceived in terms of structure and strategy. The structure of ritual performance corresponds to the quality of a particular act, which articulates a distinctive way in which any action may be performed. That any act can become ritualized is important since it "keeps us from thinking of activities as if they either are or are not ritual," and instead, "allows us to specify in what respects and to what extent an action can be ritualized. Ritual is not a 'what,' nor a 'thing.' It is a 'how,' a quality, and there are 'degrees' of it. Any action can be ritualized, though not every action is a rite." This theoretical orientation lays a foundation for understanding imprisonment and capital punishment as viable subjects for ritual inquiry.

The structure of ritual activity is often related to religious narrative and myth. In the religious context, the activity aims to recreate stories from tradition. A simple example is Catholic communion, a weekly reenactment of the "last supper" of Jesus and his disciples. The religious narrative supplies the script and the weekly rite is its recital. Religious narrative informs church doctrine and liturgy, and as will be shown, informs criminal law and procedure as well.

As a strategy, ritual often corresponds to concerns about risk, danger, and impurity; "the need to construct a safe and ordered environment;" and the "potency of disorder." As a psychological mechanism, ritual activity is "geared to the detection of and reaction to particular *potential* threats to fitness." The cleansing function of ritual activity is of critical importance in this respect since "fitness" is often threatened by pollution. Pollution is what compromises purity with dirt and disorder, and must be contained by ritual practice.

In the American context, concerns about racial purity produced the infamous "one-drop" rule and anti-miscegenation laws to combat pollution of the "white" race. Of all social transgressions, the pollution of the "white woman's purity by the black man's sexual assault was the ultimate contamination--an abomination that polluted the community as well as the woman." The violence of lynching often corresponded to rumors of such rape, which rendered the punishment a ritualistic means of patrolling sexual borders. In later times, the threats of miscegenation reappeared in the civil rights struggles in the 1950s and 1960s, with *Brown v. Board of Education* ending school segregation and *Loving v. Virginia*, another high court decision that struck down anti-miscegenation laws. These threats to white superiority represented some of the driving forces of the ritual punishment that ensued in the 1970s, 1980s, and beyond. As in the era of mass lynching, white purity was at stake, and punishment was used to keep order.

Associations between cleanliness and lawfulness have long historical roots, including the "unclean hands" doctrine, which equated unethical activities and bad faith with being "unclean." Equally ancient are associations between dirt and crime, and in early modern times, cleanliness was an intended goal of legal punishment. The logic was simple:

> Low-status persons are polluted persons. Status and pollution in turn are connected to risk: things that we regard as "dirty" or "polluted" are, broadly, things that we regard as freighted with risk. Criminals, of course, are persons whom we regard as presenting us with risk, and it follows that we often tend to regard them as polluted.

Accordingly, for the crime to be adequately punished, it was necessary for wrongdoers to be cleansed of their iniquities before reentering society, and sometimes, there was a cleansing of the location where the crime was committed.

In the modern period, the polluting nature of crime is clearly articulated, particularly in the language of political and law enforcement officials' talk of "cleaning up crime," "cleaning up the streets," or the "crime-scene cleanup," labeling schemes that characterize criminals as synonymous with dirt. Thus, when Jose, the "dirty bomber," Padilla was branded as such, there may have been implications to his name other than nuclear weapons, including crime and the idea of "doin' dirt."

This logic makes it sensible to say that government officials "got off clean" with his imprisonment and torture. Like "dirty criminals" and their "dirty money" that has to be "laundered," crime symbolizes attitudes that are as basic as when a parole officer asks, "keeping clean?" As the rest of this chapter demonstrates, sometimes the best way to keep clean is to keep dirt under control; if cleanliness is about matter out of place, uncleanliness must be approached through order--law and order, to be more precise.

I.   CRIMINAL JUSTICE & CHRISTIANITY

> *We are a religious people whose institutions presuppose a Supreme Being.*
> —U.S. Supreme Court in *Zorach v. Clauson*

With a ritual studies framework in place, this section excavates what has been designated as a "primal connection between religion and criminal justice." It supports this Chapter's thesis by establishing religion's influence on criminal law, procedure, and punishment. Christian ideas and rituals informed the common law in general, and ancient ecclesiastical courts produced the basis of criminal laws. However, some argue that *all* the major justifications for punishment can be found in older models of Protestant ecclesiastical law. In America, Christians continued the tradition by passing legislation against behavior offensive to Christian sensibilities and establishing criminal law based on the Bible, as well as instituting penitentiary houses across the country.

Biblical Judgment

Tracing the origins of criminal justice and Christianity begins in the Hebrew Bible. Typically described as the "Old Testament," the writers of this work shaped three particular images of their God: creator, judge, and redeemer. Of the three, the "judge" imagery is typically associated with the face of God that exhibits justice through reward or punishment. This role was not limited to the earthly judge in the modern world, but was also bound up with the responsibilities of making the law and punishing those who transgress it; the legislative, executive, and judicial functions all rolled into one.

When scripture speaks of God-as-judge, the metaphor corresponds to all three functions. Thus, God as the author of the Ten Commandments is inextricably tied to the judgment of humanity and the discharge of punishment. God's characterization as judge begins in *Genesis* and continues throughout the Bible when God must evaluate an individual's obedience to the law. The book *of Psalms* portrays God as "righteous," and as one who "shall judge the world in righteousness, and shall judge the people with equity." The heavens trumpet his fairness, for "he will judge the world with righteousness, and the people in his truth." God's

23

verdicts never stray from justice because "[r]ighteous art thou, O Lord . . . . Thou hast commanded justice by thy testimonies and truth especially."

In scripture, God doles out punishments to individuals or entire peoples; some punishments are even metaphysical. In the story of Adam and Eve, in what has been called the "first reported criminal trial," God punishes this couple for disobeying his orders not to eat from the forbidden Tree of Knowledge. For leading Adam astray with the apple, Eve and all women are forced to bear the pains of childbirth and subjugation by their husbands. Aside from the feminist or metaphysical ideas implicated in this narrative, the biblical story of humankind also offers a model of humans as fallible beings, prone to deviating from God's authority. This remarkable subtext speaks to the general nature of humans: Creation's very first creatures broke the law--far from being ontologically pure and innocent, humans are hardwired to deviance. This story was no fluke since the couple's offspring did not fare better, with their son Cain slaying his brother Abel. From these early episodes, a particular narrative emerges that recognizes God as lawgiver and humans as lawbreakers. The lessons of scripture regarding punishment are unmistakable, and as a result of humanity's will to disobey, punishment is a constant in human existence.

In Hebrew traditions, the model of judicial leadership was the royal court, with the king serving as God's human extension. This ideal is portrayed biblically through King Solomon, the ideal judge and monarch. More practically, there were local judiciaries consisting of village elders, magistrates, and officers. Priests also played a role as judges, and they are described as functioning alongside other royal appointees or the king himself. A monarch's power to punish derived from the theological concept of "covenant," a sacred agreement between God and his people. The model of the covenant transferred godly power to the rulers such that their authority was seen as ultimately coming from God, which simultaneously implied that a sin against the law was a sin against the deity. From the covenant between God and his chosen people came the Ten Commandments and the many biblical laws based on these precepts. Accordingly, it has been argued that the practice of conducting trials passed from God to humans as reflected in biblical narrative.

Having inherited this portrait in Hebrew scripture, the Christian Bible paints a powerful image of God as Judge. The Christian faith inherited a God who is both a loving father and a righteous judge, who combines mercy and justice; the belief that God is a righteous judge and that Christ will return to judge humanity played a critical role in the development of the legal values of the Eastern as well as the Western Church. For the Gospel writers, Jesus's entire life and ministry are the embodiment of divine justice. According to the traditions of *Matthew, Mark,* and *Luke,* Jesus's central mission was the announcement and establishment of the Kingdom of God on Earth. In the book of *Romans,* God's judgment is sharply divided from mere mortal judgment: "But we know that the judgment of God is according to truth against them which commit such things. And thinkest thou this, O thou man, that judgest them which do such things, and doest the same, that thou shalt escape the judgment of God?" Similarly, it is God who judges the "secrets of men," which includes Christians as well, "[f]or we know him that hath said, Vengeance *belongeth* unto me, I will recompense, saith the Lord. And again, The Lord shall judge his people."

Perhaps the most significant images of Jesus's judicial stature are those that describe the second coming when he will judge the whole Earth on the final day of reckoning. "Judgment Day" or "Final Judgment" is the most important event in the lives of believers, which is found in ancient cannon and creeds. The second coming is known by a host of names including the "Last Day," and "Day of the Lord." On this day, Christ returns as the judge of the world: "See, I am coming soon; my reward is with me, to repay according to everyone's work." Although the different authors who write about the Final Judgment focus on different terms and themes, there are nevertheless a number of common convictions that emerge. At the Final Judgment, the close of history, all people, alive and dead, will appear before the judgment seat of God, and they shall receive their payment for their works in the body, whether good or evil. There will be a separation in which the righteous will depart into eternal life and the wicked will go away into eternal punishment. For those excluded from salvation, Jesus repeatedly invokes a place of unquenchable fire where there will be "weeping and gnashing of teeth."

Judgment Day stands as a paramount millennial concept and event-to-come in much of Christian tradition. As described in New Advent's *Catholic Encyclopedia,* "[f]ew truths are more often or more clearly proclaimed in Scripture than that of the general judgment." Within Catholic Church history, this doctrine is found "all times and in all places." In this narrative, however, the Son does not judge alone--he has the help of his twelve disciples: "[v]erily I say to you, that when the Son of man shall sit in the throne of his majesty, ye which followed me in the regeneration, shall sit also upon twelve thrones, and judge the twelve tribes of Israel." Of particular interest here is the translation of "judge" from the word *krinontes,* which is rooted in the Greek word *krino,* and like other words deriving from this root, including "crisis" and "crime," *krino* not only translates to "judge," but also to "accuse" or "condemn."

This linguistic connection indicates how the very notion of "crime" and "criminal" link to biblical antecedents.

To the casual observer, this depiction of a judge and twelve jurors bears an uncanny resemblance to practically any criminal courtroom in the United States. Even though some states allow numerical variation, the trend in American trials has been typically to require a judge and jury of twelve to try and convict a criminal. Although the relevance of the number twelve in Western civilization could stem from a number of other concepts, legal commentators themselves attest to its religious origin. While history shows that different numbers have been used at different times, early legal writers repeatedly invoke the number twelve and tie it to Christian origins. Other aspects of religious influence included "prayers for relief," the "witness" who "swore" before giving "testimony," and doing so on the Bible itself. Jury trials were not native to England, but are believed to have been imported by Norman Kings.

The Norman conquest brought the "trial by battle," structured on an adversarial system that gave the legal concept of "defense" a physical meaning and instilled the notion that divine intervention would come from God to make the righteous party victorious. In the English development of the trial system, "[t]he judge presided over a . . . trial that was a symbolic reenactment of the . . . trial by battle." In *History of Trial by Jury,* William Forsyth notes that the ancient Norman monarch, Morgan of Gla, is credited with inventing and adopting the trial by jury around 725 A.D. The king called his brainchild "Apostolic Law": "'[f]or,' quoth our regal and pious namesake, 'as Christ and his twelve Apostles were finally to judge the world, so human tribunals should be composed of the king and twelve wise men!" In 1164, the *Constitutions of Clarendon* prescribed twelve sworn men to judge disputes between lay and clergy, which has been described as the gradual introduction of the trial jury. By the end of the 1300s, the "necessity for a jury of twelve members was finally regarded as essential . . . . The intrinsic merits recognized in the number twelve, and its multiples and submultiples, also undoubtedly played a part in the matter." This would be the rationale given later in the 1600s by jurist and Parliament member, Sir Edward Coke, whose writings on the common law dominated the legal landscape in England for a century and a half:

> And it seemeth to me, that the law in this case delighteth herself in the number of 12, for there must not only be 12 jurors for the tryall of matters of fact, but 12 judges of ancient time for tryall of matters of law in the Exchequer Chamber . . . . [T]hat *number of twelve* is much

respected *in holy writ,* as 12 *apostles,* 12 *stones,* 12 *tribes,* etc.

This rationale would be echoed a century later in John Proffatt's treatise on jury trials:

> [T]his number is no less esteemed by our own law than by holy writ. If the twelve apostles on their twelve thrones must try us in our eternal state, good reason hath the law to appoint the number twelve to try us in our temporal. The tribes of Israel were twelve, the patriarchs were twelve, and Solomon's officers were twelve.

The custom of trial by jury was a central element of the American colonists' vision for its legal systems, which highlighted its stature, as the *Commentaries of Blackstone* described: "[T]he liberties of England cannot but subsist so long as this *palladium* remains sacred and inviolate." For trial by jury, that "most transcendent privilege," he required a jury of twelve.

Despite the long and distinguished career of the number twelve for juries, when the United States Supreme Court confronted the question of how many jurors were necessary for a trial, it claimed that the number twelve was "wholly without significance 'except for mystics.'" Holding that a six-member jury satisfied the requirement, the Court rejected the twelve-person requirement as "a historical accident, unrelated to the great purposes which gave rise to the jury in the first place." Rather than indicate the true significance, the Court discounted religious interpretation as "superstitious."

From Sinner to Criminal

The birth of the modern state took place during the rise of church canon law. Much of the secular legal tradition was built from this corpus. This included adoption of legal metaphors, analogies, and concepts that were chiefly religious in nature, including "metaphors of the Last Judgment and of purgatory," which showed that "basic institutions, concepts, and values of Western legal systems" are rooted in medieval "religious rituals, liturgies, and doctrines of the eleventh and twelfth centuries." Punishment followed the sequence, being established first through the moral law revealed by God in scripture, and further defined by the laws of the church--positive law derived from divine law.

When church power began to decline in Europe, other forms of government and ideology began to compete with the old system of kings, priests, and churches. Of systems, the nation-state gained the greatest prominence, with cultural ideas and identities informing the understanding of "nation," while "state" referred to sovereignty in law and the capacity to rule a particular territory. The "state" stood as something distinct from the "government," as an "abstract" being that "can be neither seen, nor heard." Governments were associated with real individuals, bureaucrats, and leaders alike, while the state was more transcendent, and could not be traced to any being. This tidal wave of change was accompanied by codification of laws and punishments within a secular system governed by legal professionals. Accordingly, leading up to the eighteenth and nineteenth centuries, the policing, prosecution, and punishment of criminals came under increasing monopolization by the state.

The secular state and its institutions developed along the idea that government was divorced from religion, and that religion was a "residue of intellectual backwardness"; however, religion was still central in many ways. Hence, despite the fact that secular humanist Sigmund Freud believed the human race would eventually outgrow the need for this "childhood neurosis," and that by the 1880s, Friedrich Nietzsche's work had announced the death of God, closer inspection reveals that the Protestant Reformation may have directly contributed to our punitive ways, because Luther saw the state as God's agent in distributing punishment. Calvinism similarly tended to emphasize images of God as a punitive judge, and John Calvin's vision aimed to "transform the world into the Kingdom of God." Both Calvin and Luther "maintain[ed] that the state exists because of [original] sin," and that its tasks were to "restrain . . . wickedness and preserve . . . order." Hence, rather than dead, God is very much alive and present, and, most notably, in the punishment of criminals.

"[S]lavery . . . as punishment for a crime"

As new hierarchies structured society, the Black Codes of the South were replaced by Jim Crow laws, which permitted authorities to arrest, prosecute, and imprison "coloreds" for behaviors in which whites could freely engage, and as a result, "blacks became a criminalized and demonized people."

Under this system, criminals were exorcised from society, but not from the economic system, since the wedding of slavery and crime gave birth to convict lease schemes, chain gangs, and other various means of exploiting prison labor. Indeed, demonization of ex-slave populations helped to subdue and harness the people as a source of labor:

28

Imprisonment became an exorcistic ritual practice that removed demonized blacks from society, of which convict leasing became a way to reinsert blacks back into the economic order as slaves. White criminal punishment officials thus served as both exorcists and human resource managers for slavery all at once.

Two hundred fifty years of slavery made Americans proficient in the tactics of bondage and punishment, and "[t]he old slave system provided many traditions and customs for southern penology." As the question of surveillance of slaves was of ultimate concern to slave owners, the need for constant surveillance created systems of identification that would become the precursors of modern day policing. The end of chattel slavery brought surveillance technology to the domain of criminal justice. The plantation gave birth to the "slave pass"--a written permission that slaves were forced to carry when traveling beyond the master's property--among other forms of surveillance, including organized slave patrols and a system of wanted posters for tracking runaway slaves. These three innovations worked in concert to limit slaves' mobility and power; the patrols have been described as an oft "overlooked tributary of modern American policing" and the tags as "an embryonic form of the modern [identification]." These slaving tactics and technologies developed well before state-sponsored policing would begin in 1836, when the city of New Orleans created the first full-time civilian patrol. Thus, as a fully functioning system of criminal justice developed, the first civilian patrol inherited a tactical treasure from centuries of experience in slavery.

Prior to chattel slavery's evolution into penal forms, deep connections were forged between the institution of slavery and religion. For example, in the ancient Near East, slavery was a common practice and the institution had a pronounced presence in the social structure and ideology of the Jewish tradition--a practice that the Hebrew Bible takes for granted. Slaves were among the very first people circumcised under God's covenant with Abraham, were expected to live in fear of their master, and were classified as valuable property like cattle, gold, and silver.

Later in colonial America, Christian slave owners would point to other biblical passages to justify the enslavement of Africans. Justification often rested on a story that became popularly known as the "sin of Ham" or "curse of Canaan," a narrative from *Genesis* about Ham, who comes across his father, Noah, sleeping off drunkenness and in the nude. As punishment for Ham's "sin" of seeing his father nude, Noah curses his own grandson, Ham's son Canaan: "Cursed be Canaan; lowest of slaves shall he be to his [brothers]." In time, the curse was interpreted that Ham was "burnt" and that his offspring had black skin, the mark that evidenced their subservience; how and when this narrative became an invective against Africans is debatable, but what is certain is that nowhere in the biblical teachings is the practice of slavery explicitly condemned, except that an Israelite could not be enslaved.

Christianity was a primary ideological ingredient that shaped American slavery, which contributed to formal systems of criminal justice. In the history of American punishment, the likening of prisoners to slaves was of central importance. Yet, of all religious influences on criminal justice, a religious experiment called the "penitentiary" would capture the world's imagination by apprehending the bodies of its citizens and illustrating a religious ritual legalized and institutionalized by the state as punishment.

The Penitentiary

The advent of the penitentiary in the United States stands as one of the most significant influences of Christian thought on criminal justice. Moreover, it offers a graphic illustration of how a religious ritual can become the basis of legal punishment. There is no consensus of social histories that led to the implementation of the penitentiary in America. However, the most common argument is that it was largely promulgated by Quaker thinkers as an alternative to the jails and punishments of the time, which were crowded and offered little hope for reformation. Whether the Quaker motives "were more complicated than a simple revulsion at cruelty or impatience" or penal incompetence, its designers claimed that better religious instruction based on Christian doctrine would do more than just reform criminals, but even "open the hearts of [the] wretched . . . to God's grace and forgiveness." Hence, these advocates saw in punishment more than a reaction to crime, but a ritual that could reclaim the souls of their captives.

Although their use was infrequent until the Roman Catholic Inquisition in the thirteenth century, penitentiaries derive from Catholic practices, which go back to the fourth century. By the time Quakers developed Eastern State, the penitentiary already had a long religious pedigree, including the well-known model of solitary confinement at the Hospice of San Michele in Rome, erected by Pope Clement XI in 1704.

The Hospice and others like it were based theologically on the concept of "penance," and should be viewed against the background of this ancient tradition. The Hospice cell design was associated with monastic enclosure and each "inmate[] had a view of the altar" centerpiece from the cell. This facility's reputation was one of the best of the era as far as rehabilitation was concerned, and it is likely that the Americans intended their model to become similarly successful.

Although Eastern State penitentiary traces to Catholic models, there were differences in the Quaker concept. For example, rather than design space around an altar, each solitary cell of the penitentiary was equipped with a skylight dubbed the "eye of God," which served as a reminder that God was constantly watching. Inmates were given no other reading materials besides the Bible, and unlike the original Catholic system of penance through sacrament, the Quaker style emphasized the inmates' personal connection with God and self-reflection on the crime committed. Hence, the Quaker quest to save souls provided the theological foundation of the modern penitentiary. As punishment, and as a spell of solitude aimed at self-examination and soul searching, penitentiaries represent the use of the law to theological ends and reflect a type of "migration of monastic norms into society in general."

As this part shows, there are seemingly unlimited connections between religion and criminal justice as it is known today. What follows examines the broader cultural context to show that the criminal justice system is not unique in its religious and ritual orientation, but rather, that it is a part of a greater social attitude that has made "God bless America," i.e., the idea that God has blessed America, a defining characteristic of the culture.

II. THE GOSPEL OF AMERICA: CIVIL RELIGION

> *Americans so completely confuse Christianity and freedom in their minds that it is almost impossible to have them conceive of the one without the other.*
> --Alexis de Tocqueville

This part employs the concept "civil religion" to outline the intersection of religious ideals and American identity, including the Supreme Court's claim that Americans are a "religious people." This section supports the civil ritual thesis by situating the Christian-influenced criminal justice system within a broader culture that is deeply entrenched in Christian influenced civil religion.

Although the concept of civil religion is not without its detractors, including those who deem it "idolatry," presently, there is "consensus among social scientists that there is a component of Americanism . . . . [that] may be termed *civil religion."* In broad strokes, civil religion can be understood as part of a long-term social response to the problems of modernity. By linking political ideas and institutions to a network of hallowed meanings, civil religion attempts to halt the "dissolution of the . . . unity, solidarity, and hierarchy, cosmic [and] earthly, [which] characterized pre-modern societies."

A closer look at civil religion in American society exemplifies how civil ritual manifests in society, including the notion that America is "God's country." Since the very beginning of the colonial period, Americans have interpreted their history through religion and have seen themselves as being a "people" in the biblical sense of the term. This self-understanding set a foundation for notions like "Manifest Destiny" and "Providentialism," which provided a theological basis to justify the expansion of colonial settlements and played a significant role in the development of colonial economics and cultural identity.

Under such ideologies, it might not come as a surprise to learn that many Americans often understood the Revolutionary War in biblical terms, and according to one scholar, in the atmosphere surrounding the birth of the republic it was common to talk about Britain, or Europe more generally, as Babylon, in contrast to America, or New Jerusalem, as it was called. Unlike most historic peoples, America as a nation began on July 4, 1776, "Independence Day," a date that "fixed a specific, pivotal moment in the past from which to date a national [identity], and against which to assess the [country's] progress." From the beginning, then, as the republic's second president John Adams believed, the occasion deserved sacred status and pompous celebrations:

> I am apt to believe that it will be celebrated, by succeeding Generations, as the great anniversary Festival. It ought to be commemorated, as the Day of Deliverance by solemn Acts of Devotion to God Almighty. It ought to be solemnized with Pomp and Parade, with Shews, Games, Sports, Guns, Bells, Bonfires, and Illuminations, from one End of this Continent to the other from this Time forward, forever more.

The Declaration of Independence, which documents the moment, however, declares more than political independence, but also a political theology. For instance, the Declaration makes the core claim "[w]e hold these Truths to be self-evident," a posture that may rightly be seen as anti-secularist, since notions of secularism often challenge Truth in the absolute sense. Yet the American understanding of truth was long ago affirmed by Jesus in the Gospel of *John* that "the truth will [set] you free."

"Not only [was] . . . . Truth [axiomatically] grounded in religion, but its self-evident quality [was] as well."

One scholar has noted, the "'self-evident' quality of truth is but a reprise of The Letter of Paul to the Romans, 2:15: 'They show that what the law requires is written on their hearts,'" which echoes Jeremiah's prophecy that the new covenant will be "writ[ten] up[on] their hearts." Thus, self-evident truth may have been a part of American politics from the beginning.

The first self-evident truth outlined in the Declaration of Independence is that "all men are created equal." Even though some argued that this was no truth at all, the equality principle is the foundation for the Fourteenth Amendment, which would formally incorporate this ideal into the Constitution through the Equal Protection clause. But why are men equal? The civil religion perspective suggests the answer is also found in *Genesis:* "So God created man in his own image, in the image of God he created him." In other words, all men are created equal because they were equally created by God; thus, the principle of equality appears as theological as it is political.

Like the lasting symbolism of the Declaration of Independence, the country's national anthem, the "Star-Spangled Banner," and other songs are part of civil religious traditions. The Anthem accompanies practically every form of public gathering, from sporting events to official state ceremonies. At most events, however, only the first stanza is sung, to the omission of:

> Blest with vict'ry and peace may the heav'n rescued land Praise the power that hath made and preserv'd us a nation! Then conquer we must, when our cause it is just, And this be our motto - 'In God is our trust,' And the star-spangled banner in triumph shall wave O'er the land of the free and the home of the brave...

Akin in patriotism to the National Anthem are songs like "America the Beautiful," which extols "America! America! God shed His grace on thee," as well as the songs "God Bless America," and "My Country 'tis of Thee," which proclaim God as the original author of liberty and at whom the song is directed:

> Our fathers' God! to Thee--
> Author of Liberty!
> To thee we sing;
> Long may our land be bright

With Freedom's holy light
Protect us by thy might,
Great God, our King!

There are a myriad of other civil rites performed in everyday life. One obvious performance is the reciting of the Pledge of Allegiance. The Pledge accords the American flag with the sacredness and formality of a religious artifact, and one scholar has described flag salutes as capturing the "ritualiz[ation] of patriotism in America." The pledge became more sacralized when the term "under God" was added to it in 1954 during the Cold War and in the midst of the communist Red Scare. The addition was a symbolic effort to "distinguish America from its atheistic Cold War rival."

Government functions also indulge in civil rituals. For example, the government has traditionally observed only Christian and patriotic holidays. Moreover, Masonic "cornerstone" laying ceremonies have been performed at building dedications throughout American history, whose concept and practice likely traces to religious roots. Religious conviction also explains why there is no mail delivered on Sundays, since, as the Christian day of the Sabbath, mail service on Sundays came to be scorned, and was eventually stopped. This might not seem surprising since, as the Court has noted, by 1650 the Plymouth Rock colony had laws that proscribed labor on Sundays and by the time the First Amendment was ratified, each of the original colonies had such laws.

As this part shows, these and other artifacts depict the religious side of American polity and the civil rituals they inspire. This cultural backdrop is useful for understanding how a simple function of the state, like the doling of punishment becomes more than merely what happens to convicted offenders, but also, represents the raw exercise of power and social control.

III. CIVIL RIGHTS TURNED WRONG

The death penalty process displays many features of a communal ritual, and ritual and symbolism are, as we know, intrinsic parts of modern politics.
—David Garland from
The Cultural Lives of Capital Punishment

Having outlined the influence of religion on criminal justice, as well as having situated the system within the American will toward civil religion, this part turns the ritual scope onto two distinct eras of punishment in America. These eras show the appropriation of punishment toward ritual ends, which, through the process of killing, brings the civil ritual thesis to life. The first examines the phenomenon of lynching in the American South after the passing of the Thirteenth Amendment. The second examines imprisonment trends that followed later civil rights developments. In both periods, issues of purity and superiority were closely tied to legal changes to the status quo that would lead to unprecedented trends in harsh punishment. They reveal the criminal's utility as a social scapegoat, which is particularly necessary during times of turmoil and social crisis.

The Logic of Lynching

The history of lynching is a lesson in harsh punishment. The peak of the practice came after the passage of the Thirteenth Amendment in 1865, which ended private ownership of slaves. Although the amendment was a major civil rights milestone, it was followed by what is described as the "lynching era," a five-decade killing spree in which thousands of lynchings were reported in the South, with likely many more going unreported. As emancipation ruptured a centuries-old social structure, "Southern whites--poor and rich alike--were utterly outraged." The southern response to abolition was to inflict terrorism against ex-slave populations through mob violence and riots, most notably through the practice of mass killing of ex-slaves. This volatile social period saw a tremendous spike in lynching against former slaves, and as one scholar argues, during the fifteen-year period from 1865 to 1880, more lynchings occurred than in any other similar time in American history.

Academic inquiry into the ritual aspects of lynching remains limited, but not completely absent. Professor David Garland has argued that lynching is a ritual form of punishment driven by ideals of white power, which:

> [E]merged at a historical moment of unusual stress in the racial and class politics . . . a transitional moment in which older mechanisms of racial domination and social control had either been dismantled or else were no longer perceived to be effective, and alternative structures of control had not yet been put in place.

In this era, the social spectacle of bodies being hanged, genitally mutilated, and burnt alive sent messages of power and recemented social hierarchies.

Garland describes the events as:

> [C]ollective performances that involved a set of formal conventions and recognizable roles; a staging that was standardized, sequenced, and dramatic; and a recognized social meaning that set the event apart as important, out-of-the-ordinary, highly charged in symbolic significance. Lynchers sought to represent their violent acts as collective rituals rather than private actions--seeking the public authority that came with the crowd--and they used the ritual forms of criminal punishment to do so.

As Garland notes, the lynchers did not choose just any form of violence, but co-opted the legitimate form of criminal punishment, hanging. As the state's mode of execution, the practice of hanging lent legitimacy to activities that subverted the law itself, since they were used to carry out unlawful killing against an individual who had not been tried by a court.

Wrath of the Lash: Prison Expansion Explained

Like the era of lynching, the era of mass incarceration followed major ruptures in American society. This has been the crux of what is discussed in academic circles as "backlash" theory, which suggests that the civil rights movement catalyzed the modern era of harsh punishment. This section offers a fuller account of this era and attributes the turn to prisons not simply as a matter of "backlash," but "frontlash" as well, which was unleashed when it became clear that the old caste hierarchy was crumbling and that something new would be required to take its place. As Professor Ian Haney Lopez describes, paradoxically, it was the success of civil rights struggles that created an incentive for its opponents to take crime tropes to the national stage, and soon enough, "political leaders mobilized white opposition to civil rights through a proxy language: 'crime' became a coded vocabulary capable of marshalling racial fears without violating newly dominant egalitarian norms."

While backlash is a familiar, if under-theorized, concept, "frontlash" describes how political elites played a leading role in calling attention to crime and defining these issues as the consequence of insufficient punishment and control. More specifically, the term indicates:

> [T]he process by which formerly defeated groups may become dominant issue entrepreneurs in light of the development of a new issues campaign. In the case of criminal justice, several stinging defeats for opponents of civil rights galvanized a powerful elite countermovement . . . . The same actors who had fought vociferously against civil rights legislation, defeated and shifted the "locus of attack" by injecting crime onto the agenda.

The frontlash concept insists that crime rates alone do not account for the dramatic increase in punishment figures. Instead, political defeats catalyze change in law and policy and "provide opportunities to frame the introduction of a new problem, allowing the defeated group to 'propose a new interpretation of events' and 'change the intensities of interest' in a problem." For example, scholars have traced the development of the Federal Sentencing Guidelines in the 1980s to decisions made during the civil rights era. From this critical angle, the Guidelines were promulgated to strip federal judges of their historically broad sentencing discretion to shore up sentencing disparity. Hence, the Guidelines have less to do with sentencing policy than they do with the discontent that developed because judge after judge began loosening the Jim Crow order.

As it relates to mass incarceration, then, frontlash highlights how politicians and other elites responded politically to legal defeats in the civil rights era. These elites pit tough-on-crime policies against civil rights by creating links between civil rights and crime. Frontlash embodies the turn to "law and order" politics of southern officials in the effort to undermine the civil rights movement. It describes how "conservatives systematically and strategically linked opposition to civil rights . . . to calls for law and order, arguing that Martin Luther King Jr.'s philosophy . . . was a leading cause of crime. Other leaders characterized civil rights strategies as criminal and indicated the rise of the civil rights movement as reflecting a breakdown of law, calling for a crackdown on those who challenged the old order of segregation." The entry of crime into political discourse provided a sanctuary that "saved the careers of innumerable politicians who were never forced to renounce disgraced political values but could instead restate them as responses to crime. The war on crime allowed the nation to again turn hostile to racial minorities without having to explicitly break support for civil rights."

Despite the utility of the frontlash concept, it would be an error to assume that the political elite were single-handedly responsible for the creation of the U.S. penal state. There are other factors as well, including what might collectively be labeled "backlash," some of which was the result of economic factors and particular interest groups. Although backlash has been described as a "pseudo-theory" for describing anti-racial sentiment and its relation to election outcomes, as well as criticized for its lack of clarity to distinguish concepts, the term is still useful for denoting the non-elite forces that facilitated the rise in imprisonment trends. Although the shape of backlash is seemingly amorphous and problematic, it represents the reactive side of social politics that inspires political transformations. Unlike frontlash activism, which is based on a winner/loser model, backlash is the politically expressed public resentment that spawns from perceived racial advances. The critical distinction between the two concepts exists in the nature of the political reaction and the actors who carry that reaction to its logical conclusions:

Backlash is reactive in a conservative dimension . . . . Frontlash is preemptive, innovative, proactive, and above all, strategic . . . . The two conceptions also differ in terms of what might be a catalyst for their activation. For backlash, it is sometimes a policy, sometimes a candidate that stokes fears, sometimes broad civil rights developments that progress to uncomfortable levels for portions of the electorate. The catalyst in frontlash is defeat of longstanding political discourse or elite programs.

When considered in tandem, these concepts show that crime and punishment in post-civil rights America have more to do with politics than penology. The two work together, since "the extent to which the public expresses concern about these social problems and [support for] punitive anticrime policies is . . . linked to the imagery and rhetoric that depict these problems [as resulting from] excessive lenience."

The conflation of color with crime helped to reframe politics in the decades after the modern civil rights movement. The new order put liberals in a classic "catch-22," since they were fated either to be viewed as excusing riot-related violence or as soft-on-crime, which forced them to move closer to the conservative position. And move they did: Democrat politicians embraced "law and order" politics and helped their Republican adversaries write massive crime bills attached to some of the longest sentences in the world and helped to broaden the scope of capital punishment.

As these "lash" theories indicate, crime-policy punishment transcends the instrumental logic of reducing crime, and are better understood as "deeply symbolic." From this perspective, crime is a symbol that stands for other motivations, of which racial perceptions are paramount. These concepts support post-civil rights crime policy as inseparable from political agendas.

As this part demonstrates, the same issues were at stake both in the era of lynching and of mass incarceration. Civil rights legislation and court decisions aroused anger and preoccupations with issues of purity and danger that were resolved by turning to harsh punishment. In these instances, ritual punishment was a tool for social control--on both sides-- serving to control broader social impulses toward violence as effectively as it controlled the communities that supplied the victims of punishment.

IV.   INCENSE & INCARCERATION

> *In varying sites of struggle, sacrifice, and stigma,*
> *legal rituals give flesh to past narratives and new*
> *life to the residues of old codes and penal sanctions.*
> —Colin Dayan from
> *the Law is a White Dog*

There are two takeaway points that explain why trends of harsh punishment have taken their course. The first is the answer to the question "why punishment in the first place?" As this study has shown, there is a strong indication that Western conceptions of punishment take cue from religious blueprints. Although this may seem like a crude statement, it intends to suggest that punishment itself may be a purely religious form, a model of God-as-Judge issuing and exacting a sentence of punishment. That a criminal court consists of a judge flanked by twelve jurors is no accident when understood alongside Jesus and his twelve disciples on the Day of Judgment. Hence punishment reads as theological, which is perhaps evinced in *Proverbs'* well known "spare the rod, spoil the child" statements. Endorsement of punishment is not merely a corrective for crime control or peaceful coexistence, but also a deeper guide to self-realization: "Withhold not correction from the child: if thou smite him with the rod, he shall not die. Thou shalt smite him with the rod, and shalt deliver his soul from hell."

The second point is that punishment is strategic. It is instrumental for responding to perceived threats, constructing solidarity, and displaying power. In the American context, the main threat has been to white superiority, which has produced social ruptures fueled by fear and the need to maintain order, albeit the old order. As "[p]urity is the enemy of change, of ambiguity and compromise," harsh punishment is a way of keeping things the same, keeping some "down by law."

Lastly, it is worth noting that the underlying connection between ritual and legal punishment depends on constructions of "otherness" for the victim of punishment. In the earliest Christian criminal codes, the ultimate face of the other was seen in heresy, blasphemy, and apostasy. Similar attitudes held sway in the United States in colonial legislation, in the "witch" trials of the Puritan era and in the Communist "red scares." Today's politicized discourse on crime likewise tends to portray crime as amoral behavior of dangerous people who typically belong to racial and cultural groups. The "criminal" is a baseline from which all sorts of provocative labels derive, including "monster," "animal," "predator," and even "super-predator," words which will likely sound tomorrow the way "witch" sounds today.

Part II

Prison Culture & Consequences for Society

The following cluster of chapters provides a composite of some of the salient problems in prison culture today, including education, mental health, and violence. But more than merely describe these pressing issues, the chapters simultaneously consider the detrimental effects these problems have on society and make clear that what happens in prison matters on the outside.

Each chapter tackles a different area. The first considers the legal developments that led to the current dearth of higher education opportunities in prison. Low levels of education among prisoners contribute negatively to the culture, which is compounded by the problem of mental illness, which is examined next. Prisons and jails are rife with individuals afflicted with mental illnesses that are exacerbated by incarceration and pose immense challenges for the mental health of co-prisoners and guards. The final two chapters explore the problem of violence in prison and social violence that originates inside of prison. Prisons have the lethal effect of producing violence beyond prison walls, and more specifically, this part considers the problems of gender and sexual violence in prison, paying close attention to their negative impacts on the communities to which prisoners return. Together, these cultural issues give a sense of the frustrations, fears, and terror that may characterize the prison experience, and that these realities are sometimes important ingredients in religious conversion.

Chapter 4

20 Years after the Education Apocalypse:
The Ongoing Fall Out from the 1994 Omnibus Crime Bill

HISTORY OF THE PRESENT: THE SHIFT TO MASS IMPRISONMENT

In 1971, David Rothman, a leading scholar on the history of the penitentiary, ended his influential text, *The Discovery of the Asylum*, with a bold claim about its future. Rothman enthusiastically predicted, "we have been gradually escaping from institutional responses and one can foresee the period when incarceration will be used still more rarely than it is today." In hindsight, Rothman's words seem almost absurd, but at the time there was little to suggest that such a prediction would go so awry. Rothman's vision of a society less dependent upon systems of institutional punishment came as a result of seeing a reduction in crime rates amidst an active network of social services working to prevent crime and rehabilitate offenders.

Contrary to Rothman's prediction, incarceration in the United States moved in the opposite direction—radically. An "incarceration nation" emerged, as rates of imprisonment steadily increased. The year after Rothman's pronouncement—1972—marked the beginning of an incarceration-escalation that held for more than three decades, producing a 705 percent increase in inmate populations between 1972 and 2008. The Justice Policy Institute's analysis of U.S. Department of Justice data cited the level of U.S. incarceration at 338,029 in 1970. At mid-year 2011, the U.S. Bureau of Justice Statistics reports a combined 2,334,381 men and women incarcerated in prisons and jails in the United States, which is estimated as nearly one quarter of the world's incarcerated population.

As incarceration rates embarked on a meteoric rise, public and political debate was inundated by "tough on crime" political platforms that focused on victims' rights and a number of crime-related issues. In the area of sentencing, harsher repeat offender laws were implemented including the notorious "three strikes and you're out" legislation, while sentences for other crimes were lengthened outright. More remarkable was the shift to plea-bargain settlements, which became the normative way of disposing of cases, making the once revered jury trial the exception rather than rule.

This punitive posture impacted drug law and policy to dramatic ends. Crimes of possession and distribution were harshly penalized under "zero tolerance" drug laws that imposed mandatory minimum sentences. The all out "war on drugs" saw the number of citizens arrested and convicted of drug crimes climb to heights such that nearly a quarter of all inmates in the country were there on drug-related offenses. In 2011, more than 1.5 million people were arrested on drug related charges.

The 1970s also saw the country recommit itself to the death penalty. In 1972, in *Furman v. Georgia*, the Supreme Court effectively put a moratorium on the death penalty based on the Eight Amendment's prohibition on cruel and unusual punishment. This opinion inspired some 70 percent of the states back to the drawing board to rewrite death-penalty statutes in accordance with the mandates of this case. Four years later, the waters were tested again in *Gregg v. Georgia*, which upheld as constitutional the death penalty as administered under Georgia's new laws. *Gregg* effectively ushered in the modern era of capital execution. Like Rothman's claim about incarceration, one might be tempted to suggest that in 1972, the death penalty itself was facing death, only to undergo resuscitation. Today, the United States ranks among the top five countries for the total number of capital executions each year.

THE OMNIBUS CRIME BILL—DROPPING THE BOMB ON PRISONERS

One of the least publicly discussed events that occurred during the rise of mass incarceration was passage of the 1994 Omnibus Crime Bill. Signed into law on September 13, 1994, by former president Bill Clinton, the bill was a comprehensive piece of legislation that provided $30.07 billion in crime-fighting funding, the majority of which was for grants to improve public safety and reduce violence and crime through law enforcement enhancement. More than 25 percent ($8 billion) of the funding was earmarked for the construction of new prisons.

One of the more controversial provisions, which garnered almost no public attention, was a section that amended Title IV of the Higher Education Act. Passed by Congress in 1965, the Act explicitly allowed for inmates to apply for Pell Grants to attend college while incarcerated. The Pell Grant funds thus allowed for hundreds of college programs to flourish inside prisons across the country between 1965 and 1994 by reducing financial barriers, such as tuition and textbook costs, for poor students. By 1982, an active network of college-in-prison programs were available in forty-five states and hundreds of prisons. The findings of one study showed that in the early 1980s, there were 350 programs with more than 27,000 inmate-students; five years later, forty-six states offered some form of postsecondary education with 772 prison college programs enrolling more than 35,000 inmate-students; at the zenith in 1990, there were 1,039 secondary academic programs and 782 programs across the country in state and federal facilities enrolling more than 77,300 inmate- students. At the federal level, one study noted that in 1981, 145 college degrees were awarded to federal prisoners, and this number reached a highpoint in 1991 with 252 degrees awarded.

Many of these prison education programs were sustained with the smallest possible allocation of Pell Grant funds. According to the U.S. Department of Education, in the year leading up to the passing of the Omnibus Crime Bill, "of the $5.3 billion awarded in 1993, $34 million was given to institutions serving inmates."[39] In other words, only a miniscule percent, less than one tenth of one percent of the federal Pell Grant budget, was supporting the entire infrastructure of prison education in the United States.

Prison education's thirty-year renaissance came to a sudden death with the passage of the Omnibus Crime Bill in 1994. The bill essentially revoked the Pell legislation that provided government funding for prisoner education programs:

IN GENERAL—Section 401(b)(8) of the Higher Education Act of 1965 (20 U.S.C. 1070a(b)(8)) is amended to read as follows:

(8) No basic grant shall be awarded under this subpart to any individual who is incarcerated in any Federal or State penal institution.

Within weeks after the bill was passed by Congress and signed into law, the infrastructure supporting almost all college programming began to crumble. New York offers a dramatic example. College in prison programs thrived there in the 1970s and 1980s and, according to one commentator, "by the late 1970s, nearly every one of the seventy state prisons in New York hosted such a program," yet by the end of 1994 only four remained.

It is difficult to track the number of prison higher education programs currently offering courses. There are numerous reasons this information is not easily obtained, foremost of which is because there is lack of a central or national network of prison higher education programs. Additionally, because many programs "fly under the radar" for political reasons, including the fear of public or policy backlash. Many programs remain out of public view. Recently, one of the most comprehensive efforts to account for all programs in the United States was engaged by the Prison Studies Project at Harvard University under the direction of Dr. Kaia Stern and Dr. Bruce Western. In 2011, the project established a map tracking all known college-in-prison programs in the United States. The reported programs, both for-credit and not-for-credit, exist in twenty-five states, with nine states reporting having more than one program. Indeed the blast was survived, but as these numbers suggest, just barely.

The Omnibus Crime Bill was the unveiling of violence against prison higher education, an apocalypse that wasted an active network of colleges and universities that were providing important services to society. Although there were indeed internal issues that contributed to the problem, the elimination of Pell Grant funding effectively ended prison higher education and removed some of the most effective rehabilitative programs offered in prison. It is uncertain just how severe the cost has been, yet one prison educator laments, "No one will ever know the extent of the loss in unrealized educational goals and dashed dreams of freedom, good jobs, and a crime-free future."

SURVIVING THE BLAST, TWO DECADES OUT

The law did not go uncontested. A year after the bill took effect, a New York state prisoner challenged the statute as a violation of equal protection, due process, and the Administrative Procedures Act. The district court did not agree with the prisoner and held that denial of Pell Grants to prisoners solely on account of their status as prisoners did not violate equal protection and that a prisoner did not have any constitutional entitlement to continued receipt of Pell Grant funds that triggered procedural due process protections prior to revocation.

In the twenty years following this court opinion, educators and private organizations have been attempting to bring higher education back to federal and state prisons in the absence of Pell Grant funding and legislative and public support. The effect of the bill was devastating, and some scholars have argued that the legislation was a critical component of the war on drugs and poverty and the creation of an underclass. Although many advocates of the reinstatement of Pell Grants contend that eligibility for the incarcerated is the most critical policy reform, such change is unlikely anytime soon as the punitive nature of the political landscape and politicians' fears about appearing to be "soft on crime" or "rewarding" prisoners with college degrees make Pell Grant reinstatement nearly unimaginable. Although the country is in the midst of the unrelenting desire to punish, there remains a push for reform.

Without government intervention for financial and political support of postsecondary education in prison, the alternative is the situation today—a small network of institutions of higher education, which, often at their own cost or through private charities, provide the programming that exists. Considering that approximately 95 percent of the 2.3 million men and women currently incarcerated will return to their community, roughly 10,000 per week, along with studies showing that education is demonstrably the most effective means to reduce recidivism, there are both penological and public policy rationales for supporting efforts to provide higher educational opportunities in prison. Accordingly, it has been argued that education in prison might be better conceived as a form of risk management for prison administrators.

Yet, solely focusing on recidivism as the metric for advocating for prison higher education programs would miss the more substantial argument about the need for higher education opportunities in prison. According to studies conducted by The U.S. Department of Justice, "the typical offender is undereducated, unemployed and living in poverty before incarceration." Access to higher education in prison is a second chance to gain the needed social and vocational skills not just to prevent return to prison, but to be a citizen fully willing and able to participate in a community. Just as many in higher education actively resist "job placement" as the only measure of success for college graduates or as a justification for programming support, prison educators must resist "recidivism findings" as the only way to argue for the need for prison education or as the sole outcome that determines the success or failure of a particular program.

Higher education, whether it is administered within a prison or on a traditional college campus is a matter of self-discovery, the development of critical thinking skills, and acquisition of the social and intellectual competencies necessary to navigate the world beyond the campus or prison. The traditional university was established as a place for engaging with new and challenging ideas, and the prison university should be no different. Lack of higher educational opportunities for the incarcerated widens the gulf between the inside and outside and stifles efforts to allow individuals on both sides of the divide to see the other as fully human. Colleges and universities around the country that administer prison education programs not only bring opportunities into the prison, they also make present, on campus, issues related to the U.S. prison system. Students, faculty, and staff are afforded the opportunity to participate in dialogue about incarceration in ways they might not if the institution did not have a prison education program.

Chapter 5

Mental Illness in Prison: Inmate Rehabilitation & Correctional Officers in Crisis

I.   THE PRISON AS ASYLUM AND DRAGNET OF THE
MENTALLY ILL

Mental illness is prevalent in U.S. prisons. The Bureau of Justice Statistics reports that over half of all prison and jail inmates nationwide have mental health problems—totaling well over one million inmates. In California, a report published on CDCR's website by the Council on Mentally Ill Offenders notes that "in 1998, people with severe mental illness accounted for 11% of [the] state prison population. In 2003, it was 16%. In 2006, it was estimated to be 20%." Although there is no conclusive study that explains how this crisis came about, how the state's mentally ill population nearly doubled in eight years, it is a noteworthy transformation that demands further exploration.

Mental illness is an expansive term and can include milder forms of illness, such as anxiety or depression, as well as more severe forms of illness, including bi-polar disorder, schizophrenia, and full-blown decompensation. For prisoners, it is not uncommon to display comorbid disorders. Further complicating these considerations is the fact that a person's mental condition is not static; rather, it can be temporarily improved through treatment only to relapse later.

As a result of these institutional trends, the path to mental health treatment has changed. One study reports that by 2005, jails had become the "primary source" of treatment for Californians, and some scholars have even suggested that prisons are the primary mental health care provider for Americans. This phenomenon has been articulated in *Ill Equipped: U.S. Prisons and Offenders with Mental Illness*, a decade-long study published in 2003 that explains the historical and sociological contours of mental health in prisons: "Fifty years ago, public mental health care was based almost exclusively on institutional care and over half a million mentally ill Americans lived in public mental health hospitals. Beginning in the early 1960s, states began to downsize and close their public mental health hospitals, a process called 'deinstitutionalization.'"

The closure of many state mental facilities without sufficient outpatient services may have led to the incarceration or homelessness of many of these former patients. California's current overcrowded condition has stretched resources to the point of making correctional officers something of a new therapist, a role perhaps better left to trained psychologists. The likelihood of officers making medically-impacting decisions is especially acute during evening hours when mental health staff is not present. In the face of psychotic, abnormal, or even violent behavior by an inmate, officers often lack the training to recognize the difference between genuine mental illness and an inmate who is purposefully breaking the rules or faking illness.

In the prison environment, having a mental illness predisposes prisoners to engage in the type of erratic, destructive behavior likely to lead to a disciplinary hearing or a trip to solitary confinement. This situation is only inflamed when illness is left untreated. Yet even in the face of this glaring institutional malady, prisons are unrelenting in their approach toward punishment as the mentally ill are disproportionately represented among prisoners in segregation. In addition, those with severe mental illnesses have more difficulty adapting to prison when compared to the rest of the population. And among mentally ill prisoners, suicide is an extreme, yet prevalent, marker of poor adjustment to incarceration. These facts suggest that untreated mental illness is likely to result in abnormal behavior, behavior over which an inmate has limited control, and which is likely to illicit the most severe punishments from prison staff.

These vast shifts in social and prison policy have brought us to the present where "thousands of mentally ill persons across the country are being punished—not for being criminal, but for being sick." On the street, untreated illnesses and related behaviors are likely to attract the attention of police, resulting in jail or imprisonment. This point was illustrated in a study revealing that 90% of mentally ill inmates in the Los Angeles County Jail were repeat offenders and that nearly 10% of those offenders had been previously incarcerated at least ten times. With this county jail providing the main pipeline to California prisons, it is easy to see why the system is clogged with mentally ill prisoners—they are being funneled in from the jails, where rates of mental illness are even higher than in prison.

Still, understanding the socio-legal factors that have gone into the mental health problems in prison does not say anything about what happens inside the prison proper. As noted above, mental illness enters prisons via individuals with pre-existing mental conditions. Additionally, the punishment of solitary confinement has been shown to trigger and aggravate mania and other types of psychological afflictions. The general problem of mental illness is only exacerbated by neglect in treatment, which, in California's case, has forced federal authorities to take over the state's prison health services. Perhaps now more than ever the state is learning that prisons were never intended to serve as mental health facilities.

Ill by Punishment

The empirical literature on solitary confinement has painted an ominous picture when describing the negative effects on inmates. In many prisons, this confinement is typically twenty-two to twenty-three hours a day, with breaks every other day for exercise and showers. In the U.S. federal prison system, solitary prisoners are detained in a "Special Housing Unit" ("SHU"), whereas California's version is designated as "Security Housing Unit" (also "SHU"). Studies on California prisons have demonstrated how mental illness can be manufactured behind bars. In *Prison Madness*, a study that focused largely on California SHUs, Terry Kupers asserts that harsh conditions in prison have a "particularly deleterious effect on the mental health of all prisoners." In solitary confinement, "prisoners with preexisting psychiatric disorders are at even greater risk of suffering psychological deterioration while in segregation." From the earliest days of Quaker penitentiaries to modern supermax facilities, research on solitary confinement has amounted to one long warning about the ill effects of prolonged isolation.

As early as the 1830s, empirical evidence began to show an increased incidence of mortality and physical morbidity in prisoners exposed to rigid forms of solitary confinement. More recently, studies offered by plaintiffs in *Madrid v. Gomez* indicate that today even the healthiest of SHU inmates runs a significant risk of hyper-responsiveness and severe forms of anxiety. The risk of hyper-response is critical in prison since a glance or accidental bump typically must be tolerated. However, for one prone to over-responding, such an innocuous event might be interpreted as being disrespected, a challenge, or any similarly imagined threat. Thus, although prison administrations have an interest in minimizing environmental stressors in prison, the effects of solitary confinement will against this possibility.

The maddening tendencies of California's SHUs have not gone unnoticed by mainstream media outlets. To illustrate, in a front-page article entitled "The Cruelest Prison," the *L.A. Times Magazine* reports that these units are "turning inmates into mental cases," the effects of which are "hallucination; hypersensitivity to external stimuli; paranoia; panic attacks; hostile fantasies involving revenge, torture, and mutilation. . .smearing oneself with feces or biting chunks of flesh from one's own body." The report details case after case of prisoners who spent large blocks of time in solitary confinement, sometimes up to seven years, to be released to the public after a mere two weeks' time to readjust to light, conversation, and other stimulants. In this environment, it has been asserted that the ultimate measure of the SHU's violence is the "intensity and prevalence of the insanity they create." At the very least, this type of isolation intensifies the pains of prison with little concern for the long term psychological consequences to prisoners, which directly inculcates the question of rehabilitation. Although there is no research focused specifically on the mental state of officers who work in solitary units, "there is reason to believe that the level of fear and uncertainty is higher among them than guards working in the general prison population."

Prisoners have also been widely known to hurt themselves under the stress and frustration of solitary confinement. The effects of an environment in which a prisoner typically spends nearly twenty-four hours a day locked in an eight-by-ten feet cell, the effects of isolation can take their toll rapidly. This environment is known to induce intense rage and disorientation in prisoners. As the report above soberly reminds us, the most pressing fact in these scenarios is that most of the prisoners in SHUs will one day be freed to return to society, albeit angrier, more impulsive, and more unbalanced than ever. Sometimes these individuals do not even make it back out—as one study on the CDCR shows, segregated inmates are prone to suicide; in 2003, 74% of all inmate suicides took place in administrative segregation. The various negative effects of solitary confinement, beyond merely frustrating the goals of rehabilitation, can also inflict long-term psychological damage on inmates.

Deficiencies in Mental Health Care

In addition to the punishments described, the question of rehabilitation must confront the consequences of high rates of mentally ill offenders and the poor treatment, if any, they receive. At the national level, former-President George W. Bush's New Freedom Commission on Mental Health in 2002 reported that mental health in the United States was in "shambles." In the prison environment, an entire body of jurisprudence addressing mental health has developed, and recent legislation has seen the passing of the Mentally Ill Offender Treatment and Crime Reduction Act of 2004.

Yet despite such statements and legislation, deficiencies in mental health care in prison persist to the present. In 2005, the Commission on Safety and Abuse in America's Prisons described the effects of neglect in mental health care:

> Without the necessary care mentally ill prisoners suffer painful symptoms and their conditions can deteriorate. They are afflicted with delusions and hallucinations, debilitating fears, and extreme and uncontrollable mood swings. They huddle silently in their cells and mumble incoherently or yell incessantly. They refuse to obey orders or lash out without provocation. They assault other prisoners or staff. They beat their heads against cell walls, smear themselves with feces, self-mutilate, and commit suicide.

Collateral Impacts on Prisoners: Spread and Inflammation

This section looks at the collateral effects of mixing mentally ill prisoners with the general prison population. As mentioned above, such mixing is largely due to overcrowding in prison, which effectively stretches resources to their minimum. Terry Kupers' study showed that prisoners "who have never suffered a significant psychiatric disturbance in the past report worrisome psychiatric symptoms for the first time." How much of this is causally connected to mentally ill prisoners or imprisonment itself is speculative at best. But as the following hopes to show, prisoners with untreated mental illnesses tend to compromise the mental health of others with whom they share living space, meals, and recreation time; or as one study on California prisons describes, "With little or no meaningful health care, the mentally ill free-fall in an ever increasing maelstrom of madness. For those prisoners forced to live with and around the mentally ill, subsequent damage to their own mental health is inevitable."

Having a cellmate who suffers from psychosis, paranoia, or a host of other conditions is not an appealing prospect. As one researcher puts it, "[O]thers don't realize how current prison policies are traumatizing formerly 'normal' prisoners and making them angry, violent and vulnerable to severe emotional problems." The same may perhaps hold true for correctional officers, but there is little if any research in this area. It might be natural to suspect, however, that beyond merely complicating or frustrating the daily chores of correctional officers, mentally ill prisoners may also compromise the emotional well being of other inmates. Although this issue awaits further academic attention, there is little doubt that mentally ill patients negatively impact inmate's lives. As the next section shows, correctional officers receive little training that focuses on mentally ill prisoners, despite their massive numbers in prison.

II.   TRAINING FOR CORRECTIONAL OFFICERS

Stress and Emotion at Work

The mental health crisis in prison adds to the many layers of stress that entails the work of a correctional officer. Whether told by academics, the media, or officers themselves, prison work is stressful and emotionally draining. One comparative study has shown that occupational stressors do not differ significantly between police officers and correctional officers. Like the dangers faced by police on the street, threats in prison are ever-looming for correctional officers; significantly, a portion of this violence originates from mentally ill prisoners. Research is unified in showing that fear of danger is the prominent stressor for prison staff. Given the threatening atmosphere, mental endurance and stability are critical for correctional officers wishing to achieve professional longevity in an environment of high turnover rates.

Although these sobering conditions for officers warrant serious attention, prison scholarship has tended to focus on prisoners, and by comparison correctional officers have largely been forgotten. Generally speaking, the intense emotional strains of prison work were recognized as early as 1833, when Alexis de Tocqueville and Gustave de Beaumont carried out their famous study on American prisons. In this pioneering study, their praise for American prisons is tempered by their description of conditions for guards in Sing Sing Prison in New York State: "The safety of the keepers is constantly menaced. In the presence of such dangers, avoided with such skill but with difficulty, it seems to us impossible not to fear some sort of catastrophe in the future." A century and a half later, the *Encyclopedia of American Prisons* (1996) traced modern signs of trouble to the 1920s, when psychologists had begun raising red flags due to the "social distance" between the prison staff and administration.

There are other indications of the high stress associated with prison work. The website of the CCPOA notes that several studies have estimated life expectancy of correctional officers at 59 years. Police officers in the "United States have an estimated life-expectancy ranging from fifty-three to sixty-six years." By comparison, the Police Policy Studies Council reports that in the United States, non-police males have a life-expectancy of seventy- three years. In addition to shortened lives, the divorce rate for correctional officers is purportedly twice the national average, and high rates of alcoholism and suicide are found among line officers. One of the most comprehensive studies on correctional officer stress concluded that illnesses related to stress at work, including hypertension, ulcers, and heart disease were abnormally high among correctional officers. Scholars have depicted guard/correctional work as alienated, cynical, burned out, stressed but unable to admit it, and frustrated beyond imagination. So it is unsurprising that there are many obstacles to ensuring that officers maintain a balanced and healthy emotional disposition. As the training described above reveals, officers are given little training on how to maintain their own psychological and emotional welfare, even though some researchers have advocated making such training available to all officers. Although the CDCR occasionally distributes flyers that encourage ways of coping with stress, beyond this there is not much support. In this State, there is no mandatory counseling or routine psychological check-ups for correctional officers. Even though routine counseling might provide correctional officers with much needed psychological support, the fact is that few officers want to be associated with such services. In an environment where counseling and clinical support should be the norm, it is too often the exception. For officers, it typically may be a matter of pride or of not being perceived as mentally weak by prisoners or other staff; they seek to avoid being seen as soft or in need of help.

Correctional officers also have difficulty shaking off the effects of prison work while off the job. To learn more about life as a prison guard, one researcher actually went undercover and worked as a correctional officer at Sing Sing prison. Entitled *Newjack*, this work paints a portrait of Ted Conover, an experienced journalist and recipient of a doctoral degree, who details his own behavior and how he treated both prisoners and his family. After becoming a guard, his stress and aggression skyrocketed; he even began to hit his child. Even when on vacation he found himself traumatized by dreams about the prison, recalling, "All I knew then was that even though my body was two thousand miles away, my mind was still trapped in Sing Sing." Although Conover's study was arguably as novel as it was unorthodox, other inquiry has documented similar effects of prison employment on officers:

Most officers recognized the changes that had taken place in themselves and spoke of those changes with sorrow and bitterness in the interviews. Many of their young marriages were in trouble or destroyed. Some officers were so burnt out that they could not go into supermarkets or take their children to the zoo. Others were so drug dependent that they had to get drunk before going to work on the 7a.m. shift. Some were so angry and frustrated that they punched holes in the walls of their homes and abused those whom they loved. The suffered severe headaches, hypertension, nightmares. Most of all, they were desperately unhappy and despaired that life could ever seem good again.

Similar conclusions are found in Lucien X. Lombardo's *Guards Imprisoned*, an investigation into the guard lifestyle and its bipolar mix of chaos and boredom. Faced with danger and a sense of powerlessness, it describes the guard as "a classic example of an alienated worker. To cope with these frustrations he resigns himself to the inevitability of forces beyond his control and finds alternatives to or strikes out against situations within his grasp." More recently, prison guards at Guantanamo Bay have been reported to suffer psychological trauma as a result of the harsh environment, which is further testimony to the effects treatment of prisoners can have on their keepers.

From de Tocqueville's observations, nearly two centuries ago, little has changed about the dangerous nature of prison work and the effects of stress on prison personnel. In addition to the stress that originates from inmates, service staff, other officers, visitors, and administrative superiors, officers today bear the added brunt of managing unprecedented numbers of mentally ill inmates, which only heightens stress. Since mentally ill prisoners are more difficult to manage and more violent than the general prison population, their growing presence means more emotional strains for officers, which typically include alcoholism, drug addiction, and domestic problems. Under the custody of such individuals, the question of inmate rehabilitation begins to look like a purely theoretical construct; far from being able to manage inmates and contribute to rehabilitation, officers sometimes cannot even manage themselves.

CONCLUSION

The aggregate impact of the mentally ill population on prisoners and correctional officers cannot be overstated. In general, scholars, the government, and the media all characterize California's prison system deeply flawed or completely broken. Consequences of this crisis will certainly arise in the coming decades as tens of thousands of psychologically damaged inmates return to society without proper acclimation. Virtually all researchers writing in the area of inmate psychology acknowledge that prisoners are adversely affected by SHUs. What is not as evident, however, is whether any credible data suggests that SHUs produce any widespread beneficial effects. Independent of these considerations, there is "little doubt about not only [their] capacity to inflict widespread psychological pain but also [their] potential to significantly undermine already tenuous chances for subsequent adjustment."

From the purview of contemporary criminal justice, these issues, as they relate to mental illness, should be of utmost concern. Due to the sparse training in the area of mental illness, management of inmates is made all the more difficult. Thus, the system's substantive instrument of punishment, the penitentiary, is defective in ways that pose challenges to its rehabilitative purpose. Moreover, history has shown at the idea of rehabilitation has not always been welcomed by inmates, and at times prisoners have rejected the system's notion of rehabilitation; rather than submit to whatever is done to them in the name of rehabilitation, they have altogether rejected treatment. This author has heard anecdotal evidence from numerous prisoners who claim that the rehabilitation relationship is backward—that the criminal system needs rehabilitation, not they. From the point of view of these prisoners, there is no question of "rehabilitation" because there is no problem. The problems, instead, come from corrupt policing tactics, court room biases, racial profiling, unfair sentencing laws, parole technicalities, and incompetent prison administrations. For these inmates, a wholesale emphasis on rehabilitation allows the state to ignore the systemic inequalities of the criminal justice system and lays the full burden of crime on the prisoner—a gross oversimplification. These critiques of rehabilitation policy, however, are only peripheral to the core question of how to acquire success in a criminal justice that has been described as failing its mentally ill prisoners "at every step."

Chapter 6

Manufacturing Social Violence: The Prison Paradox

America is the land of the second chance, and when the prison gates open, the path ahead should lead to a better life.
—George W. Bush from
2004 State of the Union Address

When the prison gates fly open, the dragons will emerge...
—George Jackson from
Soledad Brother

I.   INTRODUCTION

The prison system, at both state and federal levels, has been experiencing unprecedented growth over the last thirty years, accompanied by a striking spike in violence therein. Guiding this explosion in prisoner population is a shift in public policy that has shied away from rehabilitative or correctional concerns in favor of ideals guided by retributive, and to a lesser degree, detainment principles. The two ideals have been embraced to the detriment of rehabilitation and practical death of deterrence. The point is obvious: the more people put into the criminal justice system, the less capable it becomes in controlling crime through deterrence. Although some have recently argued for deterrent sentencing as a crime prevention strategy, the predominant trend "represents a decisive turn away from the human relations model because it rejects the principle that rehabilitation is a goal of imprisonment. More precisely, it rejects the idea that prisons have goals at all."

Today, penitentiaries operate in an environment that is radically different from that of its 18th Century creators. Yet, nearly two hundred years later, Jonathan Simon's book Governing Through Crime depicts how we have achieved a state of governance through crime rooted in fear. In this new regime, punishment knows no limits as the author notes, "Virtually no constitutional limitations have been found on the amount of prison time as punishment." These combined forces have produced a number of complex and contradictory results, the most perplexing of which has been society's subsequent nod of approval toward prison expansion for three decades and counting. This alarming trend, however, was sounded by Sanford H. Kadish in 1967, when he declared American criminal jurisprudence to be in a "crisis of overcriminalization." Yet if one looks at the astounding increase of felonies that are now punishable by imprisonment compared to the 1960s, one finds that in places like California, Kadish's crisis has worsened. These shifts in public attitude, then, combined with heavy legislating and sentencing, are seen to be overwhelmingly responsible for current conditions in corrections.

As public vengeance and victim's rights have become orthodoxy in punishment, prisoner's rights have diminished in turn. At the federal level, the combination of the Prison Litigation Reform Act and the Antiterrorism and Effective Death Penalty Act present what has been described as a nearly "impenetrable wall" against prisoners legal redress for violation of human rights. Simultaneously, at the state level, studies have repeatedly shown that prison-acquired aggression often finds its way back to the streets and to families through ex-prisoners, guards, or other means. This aggressive influence on the outside world presents a somewhat backward political picture since this institution—meant to increase public safety—poses adverse consequences for society. This is especially evident in California, whose mission statement declares, "We enhance public safety through safe and secure incarceration of offenders, effective parole supervision, and rehabilitative strategies to successfully reintegrate offenders into our communities." In the pages that follow, I offer a set of data that documents the various threats posed by prisons to ordinary citizens, which in the aggregate undermines this very mission.

II.   PRISONS & SOCIETY: DANGEROUS DIALECTICS

Mark S. Fleisher's *Warehousing Violence* told of the porous nature of penitentiaries, and specifically, of the relationship between street life and prison life. In this ethnography of Lompoc inmate culture, the researcher notes that inmates who grew up living by rules of the street find prison advantageous because it strengthens their "social identities as convicts and as street gangsters." In such situations, a reputation built up in prison can translate into a major resume on the street. Although Fleisher's study explicitly connected the cultural patterns between street and prison life, other research has developed this theme.

Burgeoning the Belly of the Beast

Michel Foucault's Discipline and Punish traces the development of the modern prison as a desired improvement of the violent punishment that guided previous generations of penology. Foucault argues that prisons were developed as a reaction to the penal "treatments" that characterized punishment in common law England and later, America. In the American colonies, punishment manifested itself in various forms of public violence and shaming that included the stocks, whipping posts, and the pillory, social performances that Foucault calls the "spectacle of the scaffold." Public hangings and all other punishments were carried out publicly so that the offender was at once punished and humiliated, but also so that others who might be considering similar behavior would be simultaneously deterred. Mutilation (e.g., the removal of a limb, ear, eye, etc.) was another method, one that left a permanently visible reminder of one's trespasses.

The difference, then, between that system and the prison system that evolved from it is two-fold. First, punishment was previously an act of publicity, which sits in contrast to the closed doors of the penitentiary. Second, the punishment was the conscious infliction of pain and suffering on the body, but now, punishment aims to afflict an individual's psyche. In eighteenth century America, two lines of reasoning influenced the development of the new system from what Willens calls the "old authoritarian" model...The Quakers were thus instrumental in developing the penitentiary system as we know it, an institutional innovation that was deeply rooted in the ideology of rehabilitation. Although retribution was the order of the day, these Christians had a mind for helping sinners overcome their sins. Their rehabilitative model rooted itself in the religious notion of "penitence," the need to reconcile criminal misdeeds with the will of God. To these penal reformers, a crime against society was synonymous with sinning against God, a correlation that birthed the need for religious repent; hence the original and lasting designation "penitentiary," or the place of penitence. Unlike those who came before, the Quakers believed that crime stemmed from being a sinner instead of from social influences. Modern prisons, thus, are the descendants of these religiously influenced experiments in non-violence, designed to resurrect a prisoner and release him back to society healed and ready to be a productive member.

Some two hundred years later, however, prisons have become a different beast, with a wholly different set of power dynamics. One of the pioneering attempts to understand the tensions between prisoners and guards, the notorious Stanford Prison Experiment, conducted in 1971 by psychologist Phillip Zimbardo, gave the world a startling glimpse of what can happen under the dynamics of custody. In this simulation of a prison environment, volunteer graduate students were randomly selected to be prisoners and guards. In the role-play, guards were given uniforms, flashlights, sunglasses, and badges to denote their authority and the inmates were stripped of their possessions and given nightgowns. Shortly after the experiment began, the guards started to taunt and harass the make-believe prisoners. By the third and fourth days of the experiment, the guards began to treat the prisoners in a way that bordered on torture. Due to the terrible turn this experiment took, Zimbardo was forced to stop the project altogether. According to the official website of the Stanford Prison Experiment, "One guard was nicknamed 'John Wayne' by the prisoners because he was so sadistic. Yet he was the 'nicest' guy on the street, and he only made his transformation from the gentle Dr. Jekyll to the monstrous Mr. Hyde when he put on his guard's uniform."

Although the experiment has not been free of its share of criticism, the underlying events are nonetheless revealing. The events of the experiment represent something even more stark than what guards may become because they also speak to what prisoners may become. For the "guards" to be so cruel to the "prisoners" while knowing full well that they were innocent of any actual wrongdoing is quite a damning notion when applied to prisons in general. How might guards react when faced with people whom they really think have committed crimes? Hopes for impartial treatment and an environment free of vigilante justice are pretty much extinguished. Stanford students, some of the brightest in the country, could not even complete an experiment on the topic because of the vile tendencies the experiment drew out of them.

Of course, the Stanford Prison Experiment did not allow for violence against the assigned inmates. On paper, neither do real prisons, but the threat is always there. In this regard, Erving Goffman's book Asylums early on characterized prison as a "total" institution—one that directs one hundred percent of an inmate's existence and routine. As Goffman writes, a "total institution may be defined as a place of residence and work where a large number of like-situated individuals, cut off from the wider society for an appreciable period of time, together lead an enclosed, formally administered round of life." Immediately connected to this observation is the role human bodies play in the institutional drama. Goffman continues:

[T]here is personal disfigurement that comes from direct and permanent mutilations of the body such as brands or loss of limbs. Although this mortification of the self by way of the body is found in few total institutions, still, loss of sense of personal safety is common and provides a basis for anxieties about disfigurement. Beatings, shock therapy, or in mental hospitals, surgery—whatever the intent of staff in providing these services for some inmates—may lead many inmates to feel that they are in an environment that does not guarantee their physical integrity.

Violence thus looms in the daily life of a prisoner, who can never be guaranteed bodily integrity. The above passage reveals both the physical and psychological stresses that inmates must endure. Yet, prisoners are not alone in their plight. As the growing literature on prison guards shows, prison guards also suffer from their time spent in prison. For example, in California, due to its "catch and release" parole policies, career guards are likely to have spent more aggregate time in prison than many prisoners. And as a result of guards suffering from high stress, their families also suffer—sometimes—from abuse and violence.

Guards Imprisoned

It is well documented that prison guards and correctional officers are characterized by psychological factors such as high levels of stress and burnout. Psychologists have defined burnout in terms of emotional and/or physical exhaustion, decreased job productivity and over-depersonalization. A stressed person has been defined as one who "has discovered that familiar environmental transactions—customary ways of coping with the environment—are hopelessly challenged." The effects of stress and burnout can greatly impact a prison guard's domestic life, and when correctional officers take their stress home with them, it simply multiplies the damage. Furthermore, working in a prison is dangerous, and guards are faced with a multiplicity of threats and pressures at competing levels. Consequently, guards must adopt ways to cope with such severe stress conditions if their psychological health is to remain intact. Additionally, the prison system has increasingly become the new asylum for the mentally ill. Thus, on various fronts, the physical and psychological integrity of the guards is constantly threatened.

The emotional effects of prison work were recognized as early as 1833, when Alexis de Tocqueville and Gustave de Beaumont studied American culture, specifically prisons. Writing on Sing Sing Prison in

New York, they noted, "[t]he safety of the keepers is constantly menaced. In the presence of such dangers, avoided with such skill, but with difficulty, it seems to us impossible not to fear some sort of catastrophe in the future." A century and a half later, the *Encyclopedia of American Prisons* traced modern signs of trouble to the 1920s, when psychologists warned about the "'social distance' between the prison staff and administration" which left officers feeling manipulated and "as much imprisoned as those they guarded."

In 1971, psychologist Allan Berman undertook a study to determine characteristics of prison guard profiles. This research included a series of psychological tests on both guards and prisoners to determine each group's "violence potential." In the startling conclusion of the study, Berman indicated the two groups had an "almost identical" potential for violence, asserting that officers are as likely as inmates to engage in assaultive behavior. According to the author, "[t]his would carry along the correlative implication that the reasons why one group is behind bars and the other group is guarding them may be due to incidental factors."

Since de Tocqueville's observations, nearly two centuries ago, little has changed about the dangerous nature of prison work, and the effects of stress on correctional personnel can be devastating. Some reports indicate that the average life span of correctional officers in some prisons is fifty-nine years, while the national average is seventy-five. The divorce rate is purportedly twice the national average, and line officers have high rates of alcoholism and suicide. Lastly, correctional officers are "more prone than the general public to heart attacks, high blood pressure, and ulcers."

Lucien X. Lombardo found similar conclusions in *Guards Imprisoned*, an investigation into the guard lifestyle and its bipolar mix of chaos and boredom. Faced with danger and a sense of powerlessness, Lombardo describes the prison guard as "a classic example of an alienated worker. To cope with these frustrations he resigns himself to the inevitability of forces beyond his control and finds alternatives to or strikes out against situations within his grasp." Although these realities are stark in themselves, they are greatly compounded by the growing mentally ill population, which presents tremendous challenges for guards in maintaining order in prisons.

Extra! Extra!—Another Parolee Strikes

There are many ways that ex-prisoners are involved in violent crimes in society, which offer poignant samples of the manufacturing social violence thesis. Such reports are nothing new, and by now are pretty normative episodes in American culture. The story of the prisoner who exits the penitentiary only to end up committing violent crimes is a trite one indeed. It is one that happens all the time, linking ex-prisoners to acts of homicide, rape, and other brutal forms of violence. The violent acts perpetrated beyond prison maintain the brutal trappings found within, a point that can be tested against a simple scan of American newspapers in the last decade.

Across the country one will find cases of horrific acts that cannot be described without invoking the prison in some way or other. For example, one report entitled "Disabled Black Man is Dragged to Death," tells of three white supremacists who, on December 8, 1998, kidnapped and assaulted a handicapped man, who eventually lost an arm and was decapitated. During the course of the trio's criminal and appeal trials, it was established that the origins of this attack was engineered inside the Tennessee Colony Penitentiary as an initiation ritual into a white supremacist gang. In another reported episode entitled "Parolee Linked to Killing of 5 Women in Michigan Capitol," a paroled sex offender began a killing spree only a month after he was paroled for the third time. On the front page of the Oakland Tribune January 9, 2008 reads the title "Parolee Charged in Fatal Beating," from an article that describes a man with a prior manslaughter conviction who, according to officials, "raped and tortured" a woman. According to the report the rampage ended in the December 24th vicious rape of woman and the New Year's Day fatal beating of a 19-year-old woman.

The list of such events throughout the U.S. goes on and on, seemingly infinitely, yet we still have scant empirical information on the aggregate violent impact of ex-prisoners on civilian life as a whole. Still, plans are hatched behind bars, ex-prisoners are involved in violence against civilians, and from many accounts, non-violent prisoners end up adapting to the violent world of prison life. At this point one might be tempted to ask, why are more than half of prisoners locked up for non-violent crimes while the perpetrators in the news articles above walked the street? Or more broadly-speaking, what does it mean that all of them had spent significant time behind bars? Might the effects of the prison experience be a partial impetus behind these fantastic acts of brutality?

Of course, one might argue that such individuals already had violent propensities before arriving at prison or the secured housing unit (SHU), and therefore, were already dangerous. However, such a line of reasoning is undercut by the literature on the psychopathological effects of solitary confinement, a history that is bolstered by recent investigations. A front page story by L.A. Times Magazine on the state of

Pelican Bay State Prison exemplifies the point. Entitled "The Cruelest Prison," it reports on the effects of confinement in the SHU: "hallucinations; hypersensitivity to external stimuli; paranoia; panic attacks; hostile fantasies involving revenge, torture, and mutilation...smearing oneself with feces or biting chunks of flesh from one's own body." The report details case after case of prisoners who spent large blocks of time in solitary, sometimes up to seven years, to be released to the public after a mere two weeks' time to readjust to light, conversation, and other stimulants. Here, Goffman's notion of inmate "disculturation" is readily discernible as a state of psychological limbo that "renders him temporarily incapable of managing certain features of daily life on the outside, if and when he does get back to it." In an environment where the "ultimate measure of the architectural, social, and physical violence of the SHUs is the intensity and prevalence of the insanity they create," long term isolation takes the pains of prison and intensifies them with little concern for the long-term psychological consequences to prisoners. Other studies have been reviewed to show "at the very least, the healthiest SHU inmate runs a substantial risk of experiencing complex, formed hallucinations, developing hyper-responsivity and vivid fantasies, and suffering massive free-floating anxiety."

III. SCREAMS FROM THE CELLBLOCK

The very substratum of the prison is violence. At its base, forced restraint and detainment are themselves the building blocks of prison violence. Such captivity invariably is linked to physical/sexual, psychic, and symbolic forms of institutional violence. Whether it comes from inmates or guards the prison is described as a locus of extreme violence, repression, and control. Its operations are based on a scopic system that subjects detainees to intense and constant surveillance over every inch of the body. With the advent of surveillance technology, prisons have pushed the panopticon of the past to greater heights. Such violent forms are compounded by extra-legal types that include fights, rapes, beatings, and bodily deprivations, all of which constitute prison life and the lived experiences of prisoners. These realities, when added to the fact of severe overcrowding, paint a grave picture of prison life.

Intense Interviews

For many ex-prisoners who make their way back to the streets, a violent future awaits. This is the conclusion drawn from the interviews I conducted with ex-prisoners in California. The primary subjects for this part of the study are from California state prisons and from the Federal Corrections Institute at Lompoc and at Terminal Island. The state of California has experienced perhaps the most dramatic prison explosion of any of the U.S. states. It is home to the second largest prison population, with over 173,000 prisoners. The research site at Homeboy Industries is fueled by the *"Jobs for a Future,"* program that attracts an ever growing number of the more than 135,000 parolees released by California in 2007 alone.

This organization has been the subject of many media reports, and its director, Father Greg Boyle, has appeared repeatedly in academic studies, news reports, and books. Homeboy Industries has been profiled by Tom Brokaw, the *L.A. Times*, and has been featured on *60 Minutes* and on A&E Television's *20th Century with Mike Wallace*. This organization was also the subject of Celeste Fremon's book, *G-Dog and the Homeboys: Father Greg Boyle and the Gangs of East Los Angeles*, a journalistic account of the outreach work being done by Father Boyle's organization.

Father Boyle facilitated the interview process by allowing all interviews to take place on the premises and by providing a seemingly limitless supply of ex-prisoners to interview. One of my first encounters was with a young, self-proclaimed Chicano who was covered in tattoos including on his shaved skull, which sported horns. The horns were intended to prove a point:

> I put them on me because that is the mark of the beast, what an ex-con lives with. I figured that since society already pegs me as a demon, I'm going to run with it. I don't give a fuck, really. If society wants a monster, I can be it.

This individual was especially resentful of the extra punishments and write ups he earned under incarceration: "Why do we have to pay for the zoo that we live in? If someone attacks me, I have no other choice but to fight, and even kill if I have to. Why do I get punished for defending my life? What sense does that make? They make it seem like it's wrong to fight back, but for us, it is survival. Between living and dying, I choose to fight...the real trick is to ask, 'Who's running this show?' The answer to this should make heads roll, but we're the only ones who suffer. They get pensions."

Another subject offered insight into the strong connections that link street activity, including gangs and drugs, to the prison. This particular individual had been out for only two weeks when the interview took place and by all subjective means, it seemed that his re-adjustment was taking a toll. Only thirty years old, this man started serving a fourteen year sentence as a juvenile, several of which were done in solitary confinement. This time was spread over Folsom, San Quentin, and Pelican Bay prisons. Like the man above, he sported a number of tattoos, one of which was a thick spider-web sprawled on his elbow. When I asked him about it he explained:

> The elbow is my joint, my hood. This is our home and we know every square inch of it. It's ours. We weave the web throughout the hood as a line of defense. And I am the spider. If you mess with my hood, you'll get tangled up in the web, and we're waiting. We're always waiting. It's like a fly who gets caught up—death is coming.

He was also quite candid about the aura of aggression that permeates life behind bars, and had been involved in numerous fights. Although before imprisonment he had already suffered gunshot wounds, he did not know that things would turn worse once he went to prison. He recalls: "As you can see, I'm not big, so I got to watch my back more. Outside it wasn't no big a deal because I was always strapped. I could take care of myself –no problem. But in the *pinta* it's different. A man's dick is his gun. It is the best weapon you have in here because a stick or pipe can only break bones, but when someone gets punk'd, then it's over. The whole person is broken. Ruined."

He went on to tell of a particular episode in which he lost a molar tooth due to a stabbing injury, which he indicated by opening his mouth wide: "That motherfucker came after me hard before I saw the shank. It was like a screwdriver without a handle. Anyway, he swung at me hard from underneath, and he stabbed me in the neck. It crossed over and hit my jawbone and actually popped one of my molars right here. I went to the infirmary, and later was written up for fighting. They never found the shank."

The above scenario is much like that related by the subject with the horn tattoos. Namely, when violence erupts, one may have to fight to survive—even though this act might result in further punishment. Speaking on the specific policies that help create violent situations, one interviewee was particularly vindictive in his tone. Having spent eight of his twenty eight years of age incarcerated, he was resentful of the way prisons settings are structured: "I've seen it happen too many times. Why do they put thieves and petty people in the same tier with the hardened niggas? They become celly bitches until they are released or kill themselves, whatever comes first...It's like taking a regular dog and beating it up. More than likely he's gonna learn how to fight and attack. That's what they do in here. They breed a bunch of mad dogs and let them loose on society. Sometimes it's hard as hell. You can bump into someone on the street, and just like that, it's on. I wasn't like this before though. In fact, before getting to prison, I never really had a fight, except when I was a kid."

Like the other accounts, this story is filled with violent memories of the prison, some of which are unshakable, even after exiting the institution. These accounts tell of people who have been pushed close to their physical and psychological limits, some beyond.

Judging from my talks with individuals, violence behind bars is apparently everywhere, at every turn, and is often drawn across racial lines. One parolee who had been released two months previously from San Quentin, laid out the demographic mappings as follows: "That's what you figure out really quick in the pen. You got to stick with your own kind, otherwise you'll get stuck out. For real, g. All that division on the street—that shit don't exist inside. When you first come in, it don't matter what set you're from, as much as your *raza*. And that's how it's sliced up....Blacks over here, Whites over there, and whatever else. It's kind of fucked up because it makes the place easier to watch over when the colors war with each other. That's probably what they want in the first place, but most of us just don't know it."

The fear of violence is thus a motivating factor that impels one to seek protection. This very fear stems from the prison administration's lack of control of the institution, and offers yet another way that prisons create violence. In this case, the consequences of not "sticking" to your own kind can be disastrous. Although the modern penitentiaries were conceived in the image of a silent, safe and sobering spell of work or solitude, the postmodern prison is a loud and sometimes maddening place that allows for very little safety or thought other than strategizing to survive. According to the written response of another subject: "The prison is not a place where prisoners rehabilitate. In fact, it seems that at a place like Terminal Island which is a middle security Federal Prison, many prisoners come in for nonviolent crimes and soon find their personalities shifting towards violence and survival...The reality of prison is that you cannot survive without the help of others. If you isolate yourself from others, you will most likely be taken advantage of and be placed in harm's way. Prison is the survival of the fittest; you adapt to make your stay as feasible as possible."

This inmate's definition of "the fittest" is hardly a model citizen. In prison, being the fittest can range from being the most physically imposing, running a gang or smuggling outfit, or being the most prolific rapist. Here, respect is the most valuable cultural capital, and it must be earned. The quickest way to earn respect, though hardly painless, is to fall in with like company.

Similar patterns of prison gang dominance over the streets and individuals can be seen in those who turn to gangs for protection and connections once they are incarcerated. "Having made a lifetime commitment to the prison gang," Joan Petersilia writes, "the new members export these new connections, hostile attitudes and skills back to their home communities when they are released. California's 'catch and release' parole policies, which continually recycle inmates between prison and home, clearly facilitate this linkage." This ironic situation is "cyclical and toxic," and as she notes "as prison gangs gain power, prisoners perceive the prison as being less safe and administrators in less control, causing more of them to join gangs for protection." Thus, the side-effect of these events is that individuals who involve themselves with gangs for the immediate benefit of protection, don't realize or even care that their affiliation might become a long term commitment, maybe a lifetime commitment, a phenomenon that has elsewhere been described as prisoner's "learning dependency." Such dependency is also exemplified in forms of institutionalization, where prisoners are taught to depend on the prison to such a degree, that they cannot function in society without great difficulty. This was the case with the character "Brooks" in the film *Shawshank Redemption*, who after a long spell of prison life, committed suicide, preferring death to coping with life on the outside. It is hardly a mystery why one might want to join a gang in a place like prison, where there is safety in numbers. As one subject pointed out in interview, "I witnessed just about every form of violence imaginable. From fist fights, to stabbings, suicides, hangings, riots to gassings, to razor-slashings; some to kill and some to just mark you to send a message. I've seen inmates gang raped. Basically, you name it." Another subject added, "To myself, violence is the answer most prisoners feel is the true meaning of getting respect. It's basically tradition. Let's just say I believed in a cause that I would have died for. So when I was called to do dirt, then dirt is what was kicked up. What the fuck?"

Compounding issues in prison is the reality of racial segregation, a factor that often aids in the construction of super-gangs and increases the scope of gang violence throughout the prison system. One simple example of this phenomenon is the *Sureño/Norteño* split, whereby countless Mexican/Chicano street clicks are prone to divide themselves along imaginary north/south borders in prison—from many to just two huge polar divisions. Here, the "rules" of race are simplified, as another inmate explains, "I didn't post up with nobody on the outside, but when I got locked up, I ran with the Mexicans, the *Sureños*. I had to follow suit." For another individual, as with many others, the question of race was intimately tied to protection, as he explains:

> If you see a Mexican being messed with by, for instance, a Black guy, then you are obligated to take it out on the nearest Black guy. This is how the Mexican connection works. It's like a chain reaction. You know how they say, "If you fuck with the bean, you get the whole burrito."

Illustrating the raw power of their blocks, prison gangs in the spring of 2008 forced the simultaneous lockdown of all California prisons. The rationale for this measure was to thwart an impending *Norteño* retaliation that was to take place wherever the gang was organized—in practically every state prison. By its historically segregationist policies, the California Department of Corrections and Rehabilitation (CDCR) aided in the creation of such super-gangs. Being forced to live among racially-like inmates indeed divides the races, but it also unites them in the process. The schismatic nature of street gangs is reorganized behind bars, and instead of countless rival factions from neighborhoods, the swaths of space are staggered. The numerous gangs are reconstituted into just a few that exert powerful influence, as these recent events exemplify.

These testimonies and analyses offer a unique glimpse of the meaning of violence for those living in a violent world, which points to prison personnel and policy as partly responsible for these conditions. In addition, this glimpse dramatically reveals the porous nature of prison walls and how individuals can get trapped in a seemingly endless cycle of violence. To be sure, as long as the prison administration cannot ensure security for inmates, the gang problem can never be eradicated. The following section continues the idea of letting those with personal experience with prisons speak for themselves.

From the Pens of Pens

American prison writing has produced a steady stream of testimony since the early 1900s, nearly all of which is unanimous in characterizing the prison as violent and brutal. By the late 1970s, the river of prison literature overflowed out to the American public in mass-market paperbacks, newspapers, magazines, and major motion pictures. The growing number of prisoners being glorified in the media spawned a public backlash that helped de-fund creative writing classes, literary journals, and other programs, culminating in the 1994 Federal Crime Bill, which prohibited the government from awarding Pell Grants to felons. Nonetheless, over the last half of the twentieth century, many prison memoirs and other writings have become extremely popular and widely read— and almost all of them tell of harrowing experiences under incarceration.

Perhaps the most famous prison memoir is the *Autobiography of Malcolm X*, a work that devotes several chapters to Malcolm X's imprisonment. Reflecting on his violent experiences in prison, he writes, "Any person who claims to have a deep feeling for other human beings should think a long long time before he votes to have other men kept behind bars—caged." Since Malcolm X's incarceration in the 1950's there have been numerous internal indictments that have spoken of the brutal life behind bars.

In the 1960s, writings like George Jackson's *Soledad Brother* focused on the antagonisms created by guards to control prisoners. In his analysis, Jackson asks, "How can the sick administer to the sick?" a rhetorical question that gets at the very heart of the violence wielded by guards. Such sentiments were echoed a decade later in Abbott's *In the Belly of the Beast*, which told of his many years locked in a "blackout cell," the solitary confinement of his era. His description gives a step by step account of how institutional punishment induces mania. Abbot writes, "At first you move gingerly about the cell because of the body wastes of prisoners who preceded you. You spend much of your time in the first long days squatting with your back defensively against a wall— squatting on the outskirts of the filth on the floor which radiates from the hole." Eventually solitary confinement began to take its toll and lead Abbot into violent madness: "Whenever I stirred in the cell, dust rose to my nostrils. Insects crawled on me when I was lying down and I became a ball of tension...I heard someone screaming far away and it was me. I fell against the wall, and as if it were a catapult, was hurled across the cell to the opposite wall. Back and forth I reeled from the door to the walls, screaming. Insane. When I regained consciousness I was in a regular cell. I had been removed from the *blackout cell*. Every inch of my body was black with filth and my hair was completely matted."

Abbot's account attests to other ways in which punishment can induce psychological stress to the point of self-inflicted violence. Validating such accounts, studies have indicated that inmates housed in solitary confinement have the highest incidences of suicide in prison. In his case, the punishment of solitary confinement only exacerbated conditions and unnecessarily created further violence.

In the 1990s, writings like James W. Dooley's prison-biography continued the tradition of retelling this dangerous journey through prison. He notes "[s]ometimes in prison I felt like a wild beast by having to fight just to survive...many times I would think, what the hell, maybe I should just kill myself and end it all." Similarly, writers like Mumia Abu Jamal offer vivid accounts of prison life, and specifically, death row. In *Live from Death Row* Jamal tells of one man's disturbing "Descent into Hell": "[D]uring the midday meal, the unmistakable odor of burnt hair drifted sharply around the block. "Somebody's burnin' hair, man! You smell that...?" ...Moments later, a naked man walked down the tier, his front darkened like wheat toast, an acrid stench rising like an internal sacrifice. He walked slowly, deliberately, as if lost in thought, as if involved in a languid, aimless stroll on the beach. Twelve hours later he was pronounced dead, with over 70 percent of his body burned."

In another account, Jamal tells of a guard's excessive beating of a prisoner in which he hears the "unmistakable sounds of meat being beaten by blackjack, of bootfalls," followed by:

> "Get off that man, you fat, greasy, racist, redneck pig bitch muthafucka!"
>
> My tired eyes snap open; the cracks, thuds, "oofs!" come in all too clear. Damn. No dream.
>
> Anger simmers at this abrupt intrusion into one of life's last pleasures on B block—"home" of the state's largest death row—the all-too brief respite of dreams.
>
> Another dawn, another beating, another shackled inmate pummeled into the concrete by a squadron of guards."

These dramatic accounts reveal that prisoners face the threat of violence on at least two major fronts—from other prisoners and from guards. Finally, recent works such as Stephen Hartnett's *Incarceration Nation*, representing a twelve year investigation into prison poetry, found images of prison life pervaded by violence and physical humiliation, which perhaps sums up this section well: but for the pleasure to inflict pain damaging the guards as much as the prisoners the temptation so great to abuse the impunity of unchecked power guard culture so klanish defining honor through cruelty dehumanizing others themselves we know guard violence is neither idiosyncratic nor a form of self-defense.

Final Thoughts

Prisons work to perpetuate violence against civilians. Long recognized as the elite training college for criminality, mania, and violence, prisons act as a locus for all types of dangerous confrontations and explosive events including race wars and riots. In addition to violence within, prisons encourage and contribute to all types of violence against innocent civilians. The destructive toll of ex-prisoner assaults and attacks against civilians is compounded by the socially negative impact prisons often have on prison guards and the impact they in turn have on society. Most people would like to think that prisons are a place where prisoners are locked up and segregated from the rest of society, but unfortunately, this is not the case.

The sociology of prisons ultimately reveals cycles of violence. This is especially true in California, where "only 21% of California parolees successfully complete parole—half the national average—and two out of three inmates returning to prison are parolees." The current predicament poses a paradox: rather than protecting society and providing social stability, prisons produce and reproduce violence. Today, with an unprecedented number of incarcerated citizens, the stakes are greater than ever. Prisons may be breeding grounds for new forms of racial and religious violence. Whether discussed by scholars, prisoners, ex-prisoners, the government or the media, prisons are characterized as deeply flawed, or even completely broken. This view has existed since at least the prison reform efforts of the early 1900s, when reformers mournfully proclaimed: "No one talks of reforming the Black Death."

In today's prison culture, it is impossible to discern whether the reformer's reference to the "Black Death" was intended metaphorically or literally. For contemporary criminal justice, these problems should be of the utmost concern since the system's substantive instrument of punishment, the penitentiary, is defective in many ways. These pose challenges to any correctional or rehabilitative regime, and as the Report of the Corrections Independent Review Panel has unequivocally expressed to California Governor Arnold Schwarzenegger, "Violence must be brought under control to make programming possible." Simultaneously, many incarcerated rightly believe themselves to be imprisoned for acts that do not require the severe sanction of imprisonment. These prisoners reject the idea that they need "rehabilitation"; they believe the system needs rehabilitation instead.

The issues surrounding rehabilitation cannot be stressed enough. Damage is done by simply advocating "rehabilitation" as a workable solution to our criminal justice woes. This type of advocacy wipes the slate clean for the criminal justice system, ignoring corrupt policing tactics, courtroom biases, racial profiling, unfair sentencing laws, and incompetent prison administration as culprits of mass imprisonment. In other words, proposing only rehabilitation as the solution, downplays the glaring maladies that plague the criminal justice system. By stressing rehabilitation, one ignores all the unfairness of criminal justice and lays the full burden of crime on the prisoner. So, although there is a need for rehabilitative programs, there are clear limitations to their overall efficacy. Perhaps the most important of these limitations is the prisoner's own view about whether he needs rehabilitation or *whether he even believes in rehabilitation*.

The diminished role of rehabilitation thus magnifies the manufacturing social violence thesis by connecting social violence directly to prisons, prisoners, ex-prisoners, and guards. From organized gang leaders who order "hits" from inside the prison's confines to the mentally unstable being released, the range of assaults against society is spectacular and stunning. As one correctional officer recently noted on MSNBC's Lockup Series from Corcoran Prison, "Anyone who thinks that the Mexican Mafia cannot 'reach out and touch someone' doesn't understand the reality of this place." As early as 1973, Mitford noted this particular prison gang's influence on the outside:

> Unless an inmate is given parole—and many times not even then—he is not going to endanger his own life, and that of his family on the outside, by getting his name on the Mafia's shit-list, or on that of any other similar type clique—all of which are worthless, and have neither political nor moral tenets. The members of these cliques, many of them, have brothers on the outside who have been, and will be again, in prison themselves, and who are happy to settle a vendetta by killing someone out there.

Since the 1970s, prison gangs have grown in size and become even more sophisticated. Thus, all of the additional punishment and legislation directed toward gang members appears to be having little effect on gang activity. No gang reform is possible without prison reform eliminating the dangerous conditions within prisons—the very conditions that encourage prisoners to join a gang in the first place.

Finally, we cannot overlook the fact that most prisoners eventually make their way back into society. Here, the question of "who is or is not a prison gang member is important because it can represent the difference between a prisoner serving time in the SHU or in a less restrictive prison environment." Releasing tens of thousands of SHU prisoners, many of them mentally ill, creates a situation that "will lead to large numbers of extremely damaged individuals returning to society over the coming decades." The reality is that "most of the prisoners locked away in the maddening solitude of the SHUs will one day be freed to return to our midst—some of them angrier, more impulsive and more unbalanced than ever. And we will all have to live with those consequences." Stated more accurately, some of us will have to die as well.

Chapter 7

Gender Violence in Prison &
Hyper-masculinities in the 'Hood

After directing and starring in the prison-gang film *American Me*, Edward James Olmos faced the wrath of the real gang depicted in the movie. Among other portrayals, leaders of the Mexican Mafia, the "Eme," were not happy about one scene featuring the gang's co-founder being sodomized as a juvenile inmate. After the film reached the box office, rumor had it that the Eme put out a death contract on Olmos, along with three other insiders who served as consultants to the film. Despite the problems this film caused Olmos and others, it helps to illuminate the terrible and equally threatening cycle between prisons and the barrio.

This film, despite being nearly twenty years dated, offers a viable blueprint for understanding how gender norms in society influence the prison setting, and in turn, how prison culture negatively impacts marginal communities, which reabsorb the bulk of released inmates. As an account of a prison gang's genesis, the film is also a lesson in gender bias in society. The raping of Santana's mother, which conceives Santana himself, depicts how violence achieves sex; in prison, her son shows how sex achieves violence, how sexual victimization is the best way to disrespect and destroy—lessons he will bring back to his old neighborhood.

Akin to a docudrama, *American Me* dramatizes and re-enacts how this gang formed in prison, which producers claim was "inspired by true events." As a work of part fact and part fiction, the film offers a compelling model for considering gender bias in society and its relationship to violence in prison. Like a traditional documentary, Olmos narrates the scenes depicting the life of Eme leader Rodolfo Cadena, portrayed through the character, Santana. From the film's perspective, the rape of Santana gave birth to the Mexican Mafia, which was put into business by Santana's immediate revenge killing of his own rapist.

The film begins with Santana's own conception—itself the product of rape during the "Zoot Suit Riots" in 1943. Beginning in Los Angeles and spreading to other cities in California and other states, the riots built on a series of skirmishes between Mexican-American youth, who were targeted by Marines, servicemen, and civilians largely based on their "pachuco" style of clothing, which was viewed as unpatriotic and extravagant during time of war. During the riots, the attackers stripped males of their suits, and there were allegations of rape against the women. This is where American Me begins: Santana's origins as an *hijo de la chingada*.

Gender Norms in Society

The rape of Santana's mother, despite dating back over half a century, still offers a powerful illustration of how violence can take gendered forms. Here the point was not merely about sexual gratification, but was to send a message to the *pachucos*. It was a way of expressing power and domination over both male and female bodies against which the men were helpless. According to the story, the tactic worked true to form because Santana's stepfather harbored permanent resentment for Santana, the constant reminder of his wife's rape.

In a later scene, the Eme contracts with a rival gang to carry out a retaliatory hit against sympathizers of the Black Guerilla Family, another rival gang. The hired hitmen are supposed to shoot up a bar and its patrons, but instead of just shooting to kill, they shoot the genitals of one of the males with a shotgun. Like Santana's mother's rape, this violent act models ideas about gender and violence in society at large. Although there were countless other ways that the attackers might have tortured her, they chose rape. Likewise, for the victims at the club, despite the many places on the body that the shotgun could have aimed at, they chose emasculation.

The historicity of these specific acts in the film is debatable, but the fact of gender violence in American society is not. Gender construction characterizes a situational interaction that grows "out of social practices in specific social structural settings and serves to inform such practices in reciprocal relation." Some define American society as a "rape culture," where violence against and objectification of women is normative. A more radical read, however, might see today's culture as a modern snapshot of a longer historical trend; from traditional rape law that rejected the idea that a husband could rape his wife to the rape of female slaves, gender violence is a part of the American fabric. Moreover, a rudimentary look at American cultural norms shows how negative stereotypes based on gender are a normal feature of mainstream society. These norms, especially the masculine biases found in everyday life, provide the foundation on which gender violence in prison is built. Popular culture acknowledges rape in prison "either as the ultimate act of emasculation, desperation, and depravity, or the bitter vengeance of homosexual rape for incarcerated criminals." The negative treatment of women in society is the ideology by which prisoners express power behind bars, or as one warden in a Florida prison explains, "[t]his society away from society mirrors the actual society out there."

1. Pornography & Prostitution

Social cultural norms depict how gender bias pervades mainstream culture. Perhaps like no other practice, the objectification of the female body reigns supreme. Arguably, among American cultural habits, nothing perpetuates this behavior like the consumption of pornography, a multi-billion dollar industry. In addition to print media and "on demand" services on cable and satellite, online subscriptions and video sales generate more revenue than Microsoft, Google, Amazon, Ebay, Yahoo!, Apple, Netflix, and Earthlink combined. Pornography embodies all sorts of sexual preferences, but the heterosexual genre is the most popular and lucrative. Although some feminists defend pornography, others contend that it is an industry built by males for consumption by males, where the female body is the objective other that allows men to fulfill their deepest demented desires; from rape to bestiality to fetish of Asians or drunken mothers, to plain snuff films in which a woman is killed in the climax of rape.

A rudimentary analysis of porn cinematography indicates that more than mere sex occurs in the films. For example, in much of the porn industry, male penetration and ejaculation are the "money shots" of the business, specifically shots where the male withdraws his erect penis from whichever orifice of the female it occupied, then ejaculates onto the woman, sometimes on the face, breasts, or buttocks. In such a scene, the actors "shift from a tactile to a visual pleasure at the crucial moment of the male's orgasm," in essence portraying that a "woman prefers the sight of the ejaculating penis or the external touch of the semen to the thrust of the penis inside her." Although orgasm is clearly the male's alone, the "truth of bodily pleasure that heterosexual pornography wants to show is that of women. In general, in contrast to men's very visible ejaculation, women's orgasms cannot be documented. But they can be faked." Accordingly one scholar asserts, "[p]ornography tells lies about women. But pornography tells the truth about men." And the truth is not all that sexy since "men are not represented as having sex at all; rather they are represented as having power."

Despite that pornographers can portray practically any form of debasement and brutality against a female body, the Supreme Court has reiterated that obscenity is not protected by the First Amendment of the U.S. Constitution. The mass-produced degradation and objectification of women, however, is not without social costs. One analyst notes that research isolates pornography as the trigger for behaviors that can severely damage "not only the users, but many others, including strangers. The damage is seen in men, women, and children, and in both married and single adults. It involves pathological behaviors, illegal behaviors, and some behaviors that are both illegal and pathological."

In the last decades, some scholars have linked pornography directly to violence in society. More recent scholarship adds to the point by outlining the negative repercussions for society due to its consumption of pornography. In her ethnographic study of abused women, Beth Ritchie outlines the various ways in which men treated women, including "forced intercourse, rape using objects like hairbrushes or broomsticks, and being forced to perform degrading sexual acts while viewing pornographic material." The idea that pornography is dangerous for women was the crux of Catherine Mackinnon's *Only Words*, which compiled court hearings and research documenting the harms of pornography to women. One consumer she cites points to porn's power to elicit and propel negative proclivities:

> I can remember when I get horny from looking at girly books and watching girly shows that I would want to go rape somebody. Every time I would jack off before I come I would be thinking of rape and the women I had raped and remembering how exciting it was.

Prison administrations seemingly support that pornography creates a negative environment for prisoners, and many jurisdictions ban possession of pornographic materials. Cementing the constitutionality of this type of rule, a recent Tenth Circuit decision upheld the prohibition of pornography in Kansas prisons. For federal facilities, the Code of Federal Regulations states that a warden "may reject a publication only if it is determined detrimental to the security, good order, or discipline of the institution or if it might facilitate criminal activity." The types of publication that meet the criteria are listed in subsection 7, and include "sexually explicit material which by its nature or content poses a threat to the security, good order, or discipline of the institution, or facilitates criminal activity." Here one might speculate on what the general ban on pornography might imply for society, that is, if pornographic materials lead to negative social environments in prison, how does this inculcate women and children on the outside?

Like pornography, the realities of prostitution say much about gender bias in contemporary society. In fact, there are deep connections between the two. The word "pornography" comes from the Greek *pornographos*, which translates to "writing" or "description of prostitutes." This definition makes sense considering that "people who had engaged in paid sex or prostitution were almost four times more likely to have used internet pornography than those who had not engaged in paid sex." Because "prostitution" can take many forms, it can camouflage in different settings. For example, a woman who sells herself for sex on the street is likely to be arrested and charged with a misdemeanor. In this setting the behavior fits the definition of a criminal offense. However, if the same woman solicits or sells herself in the porn setting, she can make a profit. This difference in treatment might seem paradoxical to some since sex for money is money for sex, regardless of the setting.

2. Hate Language

Like trends in sex consumption, examination of popular language reveals gender bias. Words effectively convey sexuality in terms of violence, including the use of threats based on sexual imagery, e.g., "[d]on't ever fuck me, Tony" or "I'm going to fuck you up." The word "fuck" itself may relate to the Latin *pugno*, which can mean to strike, fight or stab with a weapon. Accordingly, it is common to talk about violence in slang terms of "wanting some ass" or "tearing up that ass."

Popular terms and phrases aid in the construction of masculinity by aligning "female" synonymous with weakness and powerlessness. In American cultural economics, simply calling a male a "girl" is derogatory; not even calling him a *bad* girl or a *stupid* girl, but simply a "girl." Calling a male "Nancy" is a generic example of this practice, as is "sissy," shorthand for "sister." In other words, the mere identification as female is itself degrading.

Expressions which revolve around the penis are the bread and butter of sexist speech. Phallogocentric language inherently suggests something debasing about being penetrated by a penis, vaginally, anally, or orally. For example, calling someone a "cocksucker" is typically not viewed as flattering, but rather represents a subversion of the sucker to the recipient. Likewise, the notion of getting "screwed" or "nailed" replicates the idea of penetration, as does getting "stiffed," "shafted," or "dicked" around. Other common references like "hit it," "pound," "ram," and "bang" indicate gendered language that extricates the penis to violence.

The receptacle of violence, a woman's body, is a degraded subject in common parlance. Like calling a male a "girl," references to female genitalia connote weakness and contempt such as when a boy is called a "pussy" as a way of saying he is insufficiently masculine. While "cunt" might transmit the ultimate putdown, to the contrary, to say that someone "has balls" embellishes positive qualities. The word "bitch" likewise is an all-purpose way of dehumanizing female bodies. Though a technical term to describe a female dog, the term today is widespread and is used by both sexes. Calling someone a "bitch," whether male or female, is so normal that the gender invective is barely cognizable.

Language also demeans sexual acts and persuasions. For example, when a male exhibits feminine qualities, he is told to "be a man" or to "stop acting gay." Likewise, during slavery and Jim Crow, it was common for the ruling class elite to call an African-American adult "boy" as a derogatory epithet. The gender labor embedded in the practice is obvious—despite age and physical maturity, the word intended to articulate a social order in which blackness and manhood are mutually exclusive.

Prison Reproductions of Destructive Masculinity

Building on social norms like those described above, this section details how inmates construct masculinities premised on their hatred of women and on hateful language. But before considering how inmates rework masculinity, it is important to understand the importance of masculinity and why men seek to achieve it. Masculinity is characterized as a locus in gender relations through which men engage gender and feel the effects of this engagement through bodily experience, personality, and culture. Masculinity is not some fixed thing to be defined, but rather is knowable in the processes and relationships that males and females conduct in gendered life. Put more plainly, masculinity may be understood as the characteristics conventionally viewed as desirable in men. Masculinity may include risky behavior to prove bravery or honor, or, for example, avoiding seeing the doctor for fear of being viewed as sick—a feminine trait. It goes without saying that practices of violence and sexuality are integral to conceptions of masculinity. From how many sexual partners to how many fights one has had, sex and violence are the lynchpins of masculine evaluators.

Males face constant scrutiny to be seen as manly, which makes masculinity important in the life of men. In prison, the importance is highly exaggerated. In a homosocial setting like prison, adherence to gender ideology requires the manufacture of female bodies in order to establish one's identity as "man." The process typically involves "turn out," or "punking," a form of rape that effectively turns an anus into vagina. In making men into women, the sexual obligation of a "man" is practically non-existent. A man need never worry about the sexual gratification of his partner, and the relationship is not give- and-take, but a take-only—the punk services the man, and the man is not obliged at all. Although these attitudes are extreme, they might further reflect gender norms on the outside as well. After all, this is the dominant story in pornography and prostitution—satisfaction of the man. In the prison gender order, were a man to gratify his wife or boy sexually, others might interpret it as suspect behavior, perhaps as showing mercy for a sex-starved partner. From the inmates' perspective, however, the line is unambiguously crossed when an individual willfully commits oral sex or consents to anal penetration. As one inmate describes, "homosexuality, while not generally viewed as grounds for banishment, is grounds for the loss of all serious respect in the joint. A dicksucker can never be a leader or seen as a stand-up guy." When the boundary is crossed, when a "man" falls in love with his "wife" or is seduced by another, he falls into his own trap and is said to have gotten himself turned out, a one way ticket to the victim class.

DOCUMENTING DESTRUCTIVE MASCULINITY

Having offered an account of gender norms in society, this chapter turns to the crux of this research to chart how these norms play out in the male prison setting. Documentary works candidly detail how prisoners recreate gender order. As on the outside, behind bars there is no such thing as "masculinity" in the singular, instead inmates construct competing ideologies and multiple masculinities. The evidence suggests that some systems suffer systemically from sex and gender violence, while for others, it is scarcely a problem.

Prisoner on Prisoner

American Me inspired controversy due to Santana's rape scene. The episode begins after lights out in the detention center, where the attacker tip-toes to Santana's bed and harnesses him from behind. As Santana struggles with the attacker, the camera pans to the reactions of the other juveniles; most appear to understand what is taking place, but most seem too scared to aid Santana, seemingly because they too have fallen prey to this attacker. As the assailant warns Santana not to tell, otherwise he will get a dagger in the anus, he was transmitting the prison code: silence is golden and snitching is deadly business. Or as one inmate learns, "punks get fucked, but snitches get killed." Santana's portrayal finds a parallel account in *System Failure: Violence, Abuse & Neglect at the CYA*, a documentary on the California Youth Authority. Describing a situation in which he witnessed a fellow prisoner attacked and sodomized, the inmate attributed the problem to a lack of oversight in the evening shifts: "[a]fter ten o'clock there's only one staff member, and that staff member is confined to a station with both doors locked . . . 75 wards, ten o'clock lights out." He describes the scene, "one dude was laying in his bed, another guy over there got up in the middle of the night, crawled on the ground; staff member in there, snoozing, the dude crept on the floor and didn't get noticed, jumped on this guy's bed with knife—'say something and I'm going to stab you.' Then he sexually assaulted the guy."

Despite that Santana exacts instant blood revenge, this scene angered real-life gang members since it portrayed their leader as a rape victim. According to an associate warden from the San Quentin State Prison who consulted Olmos on the film, Olmos was aware that the rape episode could cause a problem. It is nearly impossible to determine whether the rape actually took place, but more certain is that gang members saw the depiction as a tremendous blow to the gang's reputation and manhood. One ex-hitman from the Eme described the scene as a "no no" because it was not based on gang ethics, reasoning that "if it had ever happened, he never would have become a Mexican Mafia member. And if he had become a Mexican Mafia member and they learned about the rape later then "they would have killed him."

What might the negative associations with rape mean for the study of rape? Why is it so important for the gang to distance itself from victimization and to deny that the rape occurred? Further, are there connections between this sort of denial and admittance to being violated? What does it imply for attempts to gauge the prevalence of rape in prison? In other words, if there are consequences for inmates who discuss their experiences, how might this complicate attempts to understand the frequency of sexual violence in prison? Is there merit to the inmate who claims that "most men who have been raped in prison never tell anyone"?

Although this section discusses the ways that inmates inflict harm on one another through gender violence, the subtitle, "Prisoner on Prisoner," also lends itself to an interpretation of an inmate inflicting violence on himself. Masturbation is one way that inmates cope with violence in prison. As described in one inmate's account:

> You can become so consumed with impotent hatred, so enraged at someone or something in prison, you must *masturbate* to the violence taking place in your mind, because if you cannot contain it *somehow*, if you loosen the grip on yourself a little, you may start by speaking out, loudly—and end your days in a screaming, raging froth from which there is no return. You will leave this world *berserk*.

Under other extreme conditions, prisoners develop scatological strategies to exhibit power. This practice was pronounced in the "dirty protests" in the 1980s in British-run prisons in Ireland. There, Irish prisoners covered their cells with feces and urine as a line of defense against the onslaughts of British guards. By turning their insides out, the prisoners were able to mount some form of resistance and exercise autonomy. In the United States, some prisoners adopt similar strategies, including inmates who "gas" guards with concoctions of feces and urine. These attacks are frequent in solitary units and disease-ridden excrement is reported to impact the mental well being of the guards.

Inmates who suffer stress disorders following victimization may also turn to substance abuse to cope with the pain. In the most severe cases, however, inmates engage in self-mutilation and suicide. Due to feelings of self-hatred or guilt, prisoners are known to harm themselves by cutting into their flesh with sharp objects, sometimes leaving dozens of wounds on a single arm. Mental decomposition can lead to gnawing on skin and flesh, and in some cases, transgender prisoners have been known to self-mutilate their genitalia, cutting the scrotum with razors or other objects. Suicide is common to victims of gender violence; one researcher notes that suicide is "the most serious mental health concern after an inmate has been [raped]." As one inmate explains, "[t]hey rape them, go in there and rape them and guys commit suicide because of that." In one suicide note, an inmate who was a victim of repeated violent assaults, as if trying to take a final stand and assert some sort of control wrote, "I'd rather die of my own free will than be killed."

Rape and Turning Out

The hallmark of masculinity in prison is the penetration of another male, the "premier act of domination." As one researcher notes, "[a] victim may experience a lifetime of pain and suffering after only one event." From the outside, the behavior may look like homosexual sex, yet it can be the very epitome of masculinity as it represents "validation of the penetrator's masculinity." This perspective reveals an organization that follows a "dominance-enforcement model" in which "the sexual element expresses and symbolizes a previously imposed power relationship, the desires of the passive partner are irrelevant, the rulers are prohibited from taking a passive role, and sexual penetration of an adult male is viewed as the natural fruit of conquest." Prison rape reflects the traditional definitions of masculinity in society and disallows male rape victimization. Accordingly, incarcerated individuals follow the patterns of the outside, with males possessing and manipulating power, control, and sexual aggression while women sit at the receiving end. Although some violence is rooted in the need for relieving sexual appetite, much involves other utilities, which can include sending a message to rivals, enhancing economic prospects, carrying out the bidding of higher ups, or in some cases, showcasing raw power. As described by one prisoner, "I like power; matter of fact I love power. I love being in control. I have to be the dominant one and I practice that and enforce that in every relationship that I've been in [in] prison."

For those poor in power, the prison is rich with difficulty. In *No Escape*, one inmate recounts how quickly incoming inmates are sized up by predatory men in a Texas prison: "[i]f someone coming in is kind of scared or hesitant, shy, he's gonna get turned out. Chances are really high." In the film *Turned Out: Sexual Assault Behind Bars*, prisoners describe the subtle and not-so-subtle methods for turning out inmates. The process might start with a simple and seemingly innocuous gesture such as loaning an inmate a package of cookies or coffee or cigarettes, attached to which is an enormous interest rate. As one prisoner in Alabama describes, "If a man borrows too much stuff, gets too far in debt, either you fight for it and let him know I'm not gonna pay you, so me and you just gonna have to whoop each other's ass and we gonna go to lock up; or we gonna go back here and fuck, just however you want to do it, that's the way it works . . . he might have borrowed ten soups and ended up fucking out his ass the rest of his life here."

As this inmate relates, turn out may rely on economic assumptions, which, as on the outside, associates poverty with femininity. Poor prisoners who lack resources are also those likely to get caught up in schemes that force them to join the ranks of women.

Turn out occurs through raw force as well. In one interview, a man describes how he and his partner victimized another inmate, each holding the victim at knifepoint: "I give him the grease, I tell him to put some on his finger, stick it in his ass and, you know, fuck his self, to loosen his self up because I know he had never been penetrated before—it was his first time. It's on old penitentiary trick that I learned from some old convicts. If he screams rape, he had grease under his fingernails, so he greased his own self up. I'm just going to basically lie and tell them I've been fucking him and that he's been my boy."

The first attacker starts intercourse with the victim, but then his partner wants in on the action: "He greases himself up and he shows no mercy. He fucks him for real, so I had to tell him "hold up man, slowdown, chill out, you don't want to hurt him for real, then he'll have to go to the hospital and he will automatically have to say what happened." Corroborating the testimony, his partner in a separate interview explains the relentless nature of the attack: "[h]e had sex with him first, then I have sex with him, then he have sex with him, then I have sex with him, then he have sex with, then that was the end." The next day the victim ends up in segregation lockup, which suggests that he had reported the incident and which makes one of his rapists ponder: "[i]n my head I'm like damn . . . we got ourselves a rape case." The assessment, however, is a miscalculation because rather than prosecuting the attackers, the victim settles for becoming a sissy, sold from one inmate to another, as one of his attackers explains, "he just went crazy, just went to sleeping with different guys, I mean just tossing that ass up, then everybody fucked him." For such an inmate victim, the past may always pose a burden since in prison word travels quickly. According to his assailant, even "if he stays gone for five or six years or whatever, if he ever comes back to prison and someone in prison remembers him from then, he will always be a boy."

3. Forced Families, Prostitution & Slavery

Behind bars, the true obligation of a "man" is the expression and maintenance of masculinity, and like life on the outside, prisoners express masculinity by having a "family." The meaning of manhood embeds in dialectics—identity as a man cements by having a wife and children. As these terms suggest, the hierarchical system in prison mirrors the outside, which places "marital-reproductive heterosexuals alone at the top, followed closely by un-married heterosexuals, those who prefer solitary sexuality, lesbians, and gay men, prostitutes, transvestites, and sado-masochists." Creation of a prison family distorts the already socially distorted patriarchy, but it may alternately reflect the intense desire for family, or the lived realities of individuals whose own family life has been anything but stable. In the quest for family these inmates may attempt to fill the void by creating one in prison: "we're removed from our natural families, so we make bonds and friendships."

Gender constructions involved in creating a prison family reveal a "situated accomplishment" different than sex, since sex refers to identification as a woman or man, whereas gender is the corroboration of that identification achieved in social interactions. Turning out an inmate is the definitive method of establishing a rank in the prison social hierarchy in which the daddy is one who makes a boy, sissy, or son of his victim. Or, if the relationship becomes serious, the turn out can become his "wife," a phenomenon one inmate describes as normal in prison: "Like going to work and drinking coffee are the normal thing on the street, having boys and prison wives is a normal thing in here. The same things go on here as go on out there. When they go to work and make their money, we do our hustling and make our money." Some inmates live in between spheres of family, such as one inmate with a tattoo of his "family tree": one side lists the names of his biological family members and the other side lists the names of his prison family.

Although some cases are more harmful than others, the motivation to acquire power often underlies the creation of a prison family. Describing how the acquisition of boys and power go hand in hand, one man explains, "The more boys that I picked up, the more I wanted . . . it became a challenge to see a pretty little young boy come in, everybody shooting at him, everybody trying to get him, everybody trying to pull him in; it became a challenge, it made my dick hard to chase him to see if I could get him before anyone else."

This particular inmate had several boys who themselves had other boys, which thereby increased the size of his family. Another explains how he uses his other boys as a way of attracting others with material items like food, cigarettes and coffee: "[b]ut I'm not giving it to him directly," the inmate assures, "he's getting it from one of my boys, and for me, my boys get my boys—they tell him the type of person I am and the benefits that they have of being with me."

Although being the "head" of a family cements masculinity, it can be the very thing that strips a male of manhood. When a man falls for his wife or boy in a way that moves beyond the political, beyond the business of establishing masculinity, he is said to have gotten himself turned out. One family man describes the emotional path that led to his masculine demise: "[w]e cared deeply about each other. I woke up, first thing I wanted to see was him; before I went to bed at night the last thing I wanted to see was him. I loved him." For this inmate, the seriousness of the relationship turned the turn out scheme on itself and he got caught up in the process. He recounts, "on the street I never thought that I would ever be with another man, period. In no way or thought I could love another man or have affection toward another man, but over the years, I don't know, prison turned me out, into sort of a freak."

In family life, being a man's wife or boy can mean protection and better comforts in a harsh world. However, status is not static, and just like a man can lose his position, so too can a wife. All subordinates are potentially subject to prostitution, where the man makes money by renting his subordinates for sex to other inmates. Those marked as punk sometimes "endure years of sexual slavery and torture." One inmate describes his own experience at the hands of his man: "[i]t happens all the time. They could pimp me out and make, you know, triple, make more money than they've invested," or as another attests, "they either want you for your money or your ass." Sometimes inmates will settle for drugs, as described by an inmate who tells of life as a teenager in jail and prison in Florida, where he extorts his homosexual cellmate's prescription Demoral. In his situation, he became a "man" through force of intimidation, even though no violence was involved:

> I had a good life for a week or so. I'd never had a servant before, lot less one that hung onto my every word and was thrilled if I just talked halfway nice to him/her. I was beginning to see that the rules were different in here than on the street. Outside these walls, weaker people have an even say with the stronger and the laws enforced that. But here the stronger ruled the weak, and the weak had to be ruled otherwise they'd just do what ever they wanted, all of which involved disrespecting their superiors. Besides, the weak enjoy being controlled; it takes away their sense of responsibility. It's as if you're the Daddy and they're the kid, when problems arise, your say is final. Sometimes you might have to beat them a little just to remind them of their place, but for the most part, it's understood who runs things.

As this inmate's language suggests, an emasculated male is called "she" or "her" to indicate inferior status. The extreme of subordination is sex enslavement, which may be distinguished from prostitution since there is nothing gained by a slave "lent out" for the purposes of sexual assault by other inmates. Boys and sissies typically obtain material rewards for their services, but slaves get nothing; instead, a man might lend out the slave to an individual or group, in some cases as a form of punishment. Some slaves are forced to perform multiple sex acts in a day, and it is not uncommon for an individual to perform oral sex on or be sodomized by a line-up of inmates in a single session.

Guard on Prisoner

When he entered Angola prison back in the 1970s, Billy Wayne Sinclair recounts how guard and staff attitudes helped perpetuate toxic ideas about gender. As the driver carrying Sinclair and the other new inmates arrives, he jokes, "I've got five fresh fish in here," referring to the inmates. Without hesitation the uniformed guard looks at the group and retorts, "[t]hat young one in there is going to make some dude happy tonight." Although such language may seem unbelievable to an outsider, for prisoners it is anything but. Later that night Sinclair witnesses the same inmate attacked at knifepoint, "while [a] guard stood at his post, no more than a hundred feet from the attack, watching." Even though these events are decades removed, according to the data, guards not only make such statements and ignore such attacks, they even orchestrate them.

Direct Assaults & Orchestral Maneuvers in the Dark

Violence perpetuated against inmates by guards includes both the sexual and gendered variety. In 2005, the Bureau of Justice Statistics reported that "42% of allegations [of sexual violence] involved staff sexual misconduct." Although direct sexual assaults are common, there are also gendered modes of behavior such as the old "Tucker telephone" in Arkansas prisons. This form of abuse consisted of a naked inmate being strapped to a table with electrodes attached to his foot and genitals. Electrical charges were then sent through his body, and in some cases "long distance" calls would render the prisoner unconscious. Other forms of violence surface in times of crisis like the Attica Riots, where prisoners were stripped naked and beaten in the genitals, including one whom guards caught and applied burning cigarettes to his genitals.

The classic set of letters penned by Jack Henry Abbott describes a beating he takes in a strip search:

> I am thrown down the stairs, and I lie on the floor, waiting. My nose is bleeding and my ears are ringing from blows to my skull.
> "Get up!"
> Immediately I am knocked down again.
> "Strip!"

I stand, shakily, and shed my clothing. His hands are pulling my hair, but I dare not move.
"Turn around!"
I turn.
"Bend over!"
I bend over. He inspects my anus and my private parts, and I watch, anxiously, hoping with all my might he does not hurt me there.

This episode resonates with a transgender inmate's account from *Cruel and Unusual*, which describes a sergeant's assault in similar circumstances:

> I worked outside the fence, I was minimum security. On the way out one morning, the sergeant had frisked me once and then he decided he was going to do it again in front of everybody else. He got behind me and started feeling my breasts and squeezing my nipples with his fingers and rolling them around and grabbing my butt and squeezing it and patting it and just acting like a pervert. And there's nothing you can do but just stand there and take it. I had wrote a grievance on that and that's when they came out to the break yard—they told me that I was never going to leave the camp, I was never going to leave the prison alive.

In another account, an inmate in Florida relives how he was strip-searched by a sergeant after visiting hours. After taking him to the "shakedown room," the sergeant masturbated at the inmate from inside the control room. This was not an isolated episode, as later the sergeant would expose himself to the inmate and demand service:

> [H]e looks at me and tells me to lick it—his exact words . . . I started pleading with him . . . he put his hand on my head and tells me to lick it, and he's using an authoritative tone ordering me to lick it. He forced my head down there, and he had his other hand down there. He ejaculated on my face and my mouth.

Detailing how he resisted from fighting back, the inmate notes the costs of defending oneself in prison: "If I'm ever placed in this same situation in what we refer to as the "free world," I could have simply walked away or if he would have gone to put his hands on me I could have defended myself, could have broken his jaw . . . but when it's somebody standing in a uniform, and all you see is sergeant stripes and a whistle hanging there and an I.D., and they are the people who run your life—I didn't know what to do. Only thing I kept thinking was another 15 years if I hurt this man, I'm going to be in prison another 15 years. Nobody's going to believe me, nobody is ever going to believe this. If he's capable of doing something like that, he could pull drugs out of his pocket and say "look what I found on you," rip his shirt and say "'you just assaulted me.'"

This inmate's story not only illustrates the disparity in power between inmates and guards, but also how sometimes inmates achieve some semblance of justice. This inmate eventually cooperated with prison officials to set up a video-sting operation on the guard, which recorded the sergeant exposing himself again to the inmate. Although the guard lost his job as a result of the sting, this was insufficient punishment from the inmate's perspective. More troubling was that the guard got no jail or prison, and was still a danger on the street. This inmate's story supports research that suggests prison officials use their authority to gain sexual contact with inmates.

Intense fear of attack can lead to unanticipated outcomes, and inmates have been known to achieve erections due to the attack of guards. Abbott tells in dramatic fashion: "I was so constantly and arbitrarily attacked in my cell there, after a while my desire for physical relief was so powerful and all-pervading that when the guards finally would leave off the attack and exit my cell, I would sometimes achieve an erection out of despair and pain. I have in those conditions had to masturbate to relieve myself, but not masturbate with any vision in my mind, my imagination. The pure physical act of caressing the penis after numberless exposures to attack is enough. It is entirely a physical thing, entirely involuntary."

In addition to direct confrontation, guards foment violence by orchestrating attacks by other inmates. Although reports have documented guards promoting "gladiator fights" among inmates, there is equally compelling evidence showing that guards arrange rape rooms for "booty bandits," known rapists, to have access to inmates. Perhaps the most famous case comes from Corcoran State Prison in California, where one such rapist testified that guards knew about his reputation and used him regularly to "punish" insubordinate inmates. There are even instances where staff members forced prisoners to have sex with one another. In another case, a Michigan inmate filed an affidavit citing a guard who threatened to rape the inmate's daughter and distributed her home address to other inmates.

Turning a Blind Eye

Guards tend to subscribe to the same code of silence that governs prisoner subculture, and those who break ranks and report the abuses of fellow staff may be shunned or harmed. Even though prisons prohibit consensual sex and issue disciplinary sanctions for violations, the acts are a widespread occurrence behind bars, suggesting that guards selectively use their authority to report violations. One might speculate that guards may use this same discretion when it comes to non-consensual behavior (or at the very least may misinterpret the acts), "try to avoid embarrassing confrontation with inmates," or simply fail to define certain acts as rape simply because there is no knife to the throat.

Perhaps one of the most frequent complaints is that guards ignore victimization and allow attacks to take place in their presence. In both research and formal grievances, inmates report that guards fail to respond to pleas for protection against violence. Sometimes the behavior arises from neglect, but other times procedural barriers prevent aid, such as when guards cannot compile enough credible evidence to grant an inmate protective custody. When guards turn a blind eye to the problem, ignore it outright, or are unable to respond, inmates report feelings of desperation and hopelessness. One account offers candid testimony of this problem at its worst:

> From my angle, I could make out someone laid over a bunk with his hands tied to the bunk rails. A sock had been shoved in his mouth and his pants were pulled down to his knees that were planted on the concrete floor. Various characters were taking turns corn-holing him from behind. When the Dorm officer came through for count time, everyone scrambled back to their bunks leaving the victim in this user friendly position. The guard stopped for a moment, took in the situation then continued counting. Once the guard was gone, the butt party was continued.

Like the way that skepticism attaches to rape victims on the outside, inmates are similarly doubted. Rape perpetuated against women on the outside often entails the victim overcoming presumptions that she must be lying or that the sex was consensual.

Likewise, in some facilities, homosexuals, queens, and others are assumed to be in a state of permanent consent. Others assume that if a "man" cannot fight off his aggressors, he must have "wanted it," typically designated by the creed "fuck or fight." Such was the conclusion of a psychologist in the infamous Rodney Hulin Jr. case, who is reported to have told the victim's mother after multiple rapes, "he probably likes it." Lawyers for Texas Prisoners attorney Donna Brorby describe how this attitude guides prison officials in their work: "[y]ou see this pattern in some of the investigations that express this disbelief that a gay who did not want to have anal sex could be a victim of a rape—that somehow if it happened it was because the guy wanted it." This indeed captures the sentiment of one guard who chides a victim of a gangbang—"*I thought you liked dick.*"

For homosexual and transgender inmates, the lack of staff response is acute. In an MSNBC documentary, one inmate describes how homosexuals experience "disrespect day in and day out," both from inmates and guards. Another inmate adds that negative attitudes run up to the highest levels of administration:

> Three days after I was out in the prison, I was in my cell and the warden came into my cell and he says "do you have a penis or a vagina between your legs?" I says I still have a penis. He says, "let me see." So I had to drop my drawers and show him. Then he says "you know we're not going to treat you here. We don't recognize transsexuals as a serious medical need and were not going to treat you." Then he says, "more than likely you'll wind up killing yourself."

Although the attitudes by guards and administrative staff may contribute to gender violence, sometimes guards are at the receiving end of the same. Inmates have homosexually raped guards, most evidently in times of riot. There are also reports by female guards who have suffered victimization at the hands of male inmates.

GHETTO GIRLS AND BOYS BEWARE

Santana's release from prison brings this chapter's thesis full circle; namely, it shows that marginal communities disproportionately absorb the post-prison stress disorders caused by gender violence in prison. Research indicates that Santana's relocation pattern is not random and that the vast majority of inmates eventually return to the communities where they committed the crime or where they have family or friends: neighborhoods where crime rates and drug use are high and standards of living low. By the time Santana exits prison, he has spent his entire adult life as a ward of the state, and as if on cue, he returns to his old neighborhood.

Santana soon meets a girl from the same community, the cousin of his brother's best friend, and they begin dating. In dramatic cinematography that portrays their first intimate encounter, the film alternates with happenings back inside prison. Behind bars, members of his gang have invited an Italian mafioso's son to drink prison-made alcohol, a set up to retaliate against the mafioso. As the couple begin exchanging affections, the film pans to the prison where the gang appears to befriend the inmate, getting him tipsy and telling jokes in benign camaraderie. As the passion grows between Santana and the woman, he has a look of confusion, which she realizes is due to the fact that he has never been with a woman before. But back in prison, the gang is anything but confused, and after the inmate is drunk, they joke that things will get better as soon as the "broad" arrives. The mafioso's son responds, "who's the broad?" "[y]ou," says one of the Eme members as they seize him and begin their attack, spreading his legs and bending him over a bag of grains to muffle his screams and cries. As one of the men prepares himself to sodomize the inmate, the film returns to Santana's date, which has taken a stark turn. In bed, he eventually starts to become violent with the woman and forces her into the same compromised position as the victim in prison. Oblivious to her cries and screams, Santana's prison instincts take over as if he has done this before. At the moment Santana reaches orgasm, the prisoners reach their own climax by stabbing a dagger into their victim's anus.

The point is clear—Santanta is merely doing what he learned to do in prison, and what his friends are still doing. It is the model of one who has been "prisonized" or "institutionalized" to prison culture in a way that disrupts the potential for successful reintegration. Although Santana's encounter starts off as consensual, it soon escalates into rape, a colossal failure in the transition from prison life to the outside world. Although the woman fights back and eventually escapes his grasp, the inmate back in prison is not so lucky. The prison attack was not merely a killing, but a display of destructive masculinity, a symbolic ritual that accomplishes more than merely murder.

Santana's situation resounds with reports about the negative long-term consequences for both perpetrators and victims of prison violence. First and foremost is the contention that due to the frustration of being raped, some may turn their rage on the outside world and rape someone else in an attempt to regain their manhood. Due to their victimization, some prisoners leave confinement more antisocial than when they entered, and this sets the stage for sexual and other crimes. Congress used a similar line of reasoning when it created the Prison Rape Elimination Act (PREA), which asserts that "prison rape endangers the public safety by making brutalized inmates more likely to commit crimes when they are released." This view also comports with the idea that inmates who adapt to the "sexually dysfunctional world of prison may guarantee a degree of social marginalization upon release that will compromise future relationships and long-term social adjustment in free society." More specifically, Santana illustrates the position that perpetrators of sexual violence may be sexually violent with females on the outside when released.

The spatial designation, "outside," may distort the issue because it is not society at large that is made vulnerable by this phenomenon, but rather, the burden is felt mostly by poor minority communities. Although this chapter on gender violence represents one set of problems resulting from structural failures, there are others. Closely related is the spread of HIV/AIDs and other sexually transmitted diseases which tie directly to this thesis. Infection in U.S. prisons is more than three times that of the general population with three- fourths of AIDs-related deaths suffered by African Americans. Victimization in prison is an urgent public health issue that spatially concentrates on inner city slums. Furthermore, masculinity norms may complicate matters since a man who is raped in prison and who then returns home to a girlfriend or wife may not be forthcoming with information about the assault, which may put the community at further risk.

That returning prisoners increase the likelihood of transmission to others in the community might make one question why condoms are not allowed in prison. Beyond, one might wonder why homosexual sex in prison is banned in the first place. Although the answers may seem self-evident, closer scrutiny shows that prison, as an institution, also hates homosexuality. This may have something to do with why sex among inmates is proscribed behind bars, and even though some facilities permit conjugal visits, historically these have been limited to heterosexual unions. California became the first state to allow for same-sex visits in 2007, yet for almost a century, carefully worded rules afforded no room for same-sex conjugal visits since same sex marriage unions were disallowed; hence what appears outwardly as merely penal policy is really a cultural code of contempt for homosexual-sex.

PROSPECTS FOR DAMAGE CONTROL

The arguments advanced in this chapter point to a number of problems resulting from cycles of destructive masculinity and conclude by considering how legal and cultural interventions may mitigate gender violence in prison, and perhaps, in general. Although the focus of this work has been on gender violence, the structural arguments herein lend themselves to other points of analysis, including how prisons complicate economics, family life, and public health. As mentioned, the banning of condoms may compromise public health by promoting the spread of disease. Yet in some prison systems, condoms are highly prized contraband, whose possession results in disciplinary punishment. Structural failures also affect the mental health of marginal communities. Punishments like solitary confinement are known to exacerbate mental illness, which eventually makes its way back to communities that lack mental health treatment. Further, an economics-based analysis might elaborate on how seemingly innocuous policies, from making outgoing telephone calls "collect" to for-profit canteen services to counting prisoners for tax purposes, suck money from inmates, their families, and communities. These other potential avenues of analysis dramatize how collateral consequences of imprisonment disproportionately impact marginal communities.

Community Interventions

Legal reform is a powerful means of scaling back the problem of gender violence in prison, yet social action plays a critical role as well. Although the law can help address the institutional causes of rape, it cannot change deeply entrenched social norms without the will of the people. Rather, law and culture must work together comprehensively to remedy the issue inside and out.

Although it might sound counter-intuitive, inmates may play a role in deconstructing destructive masculinity. In the same way the prison code of silence is based on destructive varieties of "honor" for its sustenance, inmates might foster a culture of intervention over silence. Of course, in prison intervention has proven to be a deadly business for decades. For example, one inmate described a "tug of consciousness" when he was faced with the choice of saving another prisoner, Parks, from sex slavery by accepting him as a gift from another inmate. The inmate recalls his vexation about whether the gift might jeopardize his own well-being:

I was not homosexual and didn't want to be part of the subculture with an inherent potential for violence. Had I taken Parks under my wing, I would have been forced to fight, even kill, to protect him from predatory homosexual studs who wanted him. In prison, sex is property. An inmate has an absolute duty to protect his property or he is considered weak—a condition that inevitably evokes a lethal challenge.

From this perspective, the inmate's solution was simple: not having property was easier than the extra exposure to violence. But, hypothetically speaking, what if he would have chosen differently? Might it have prevented the attack he witnessed later that night as several other inmates laid claim:

I lay on my bunk powerless to help Parks as the rapist got in the bunk beside him.

"Watch for me," he said, undressing. "If the Man comes in, stall him."

"Turn over bitch," he demanded.
I imagined Parks' face twitching uncontrollably as fingers packed in cold Vaseline. He screamed as his attacker penetrated him in a single thrust, driving into the boy's rectum, relishing the power it gave him.

"Shake back, bitch," the attacker moaned. "Give daddy a wiggle."

Parks felt a searing pain as one of the other inmates pressed a lit cigarette against his flesh.

"Give your daddy a wiggle, bitch" he demanded, choking off a laugh," or I'll keep this fire on your ass all night."

Parks started crying as he pushed his buttocks back and wiggled his ass against his attacker . . . he knew his life would never be the same again.

Although the author did not "want to be a part" of this culture, his omission does not save him from exposure to the violence, which according to one researcher is one of the most frequently reported traumas antecedent to post-traumatic stress disorders.

Religion may also play a role in lessening violence in prison. Specifically, Muslim groups in prison take a firm stance on homosexuality and Muslim prisoners negate the culture of rape through the Islamic alternative to sexual violence:

> The Islamic regime acquires a double significance in its strict opposition to homosexuality . . . Sexual possession, domination, and submission represent forms of "hard currency" in prison. Thus by asserting the distinction between halal and haram, between what is permitted and what is forbidden, the Muslim community simultaneously follows Islamic laws and negates one of the defining characteristics of prison life.

As early as the 1970s, one inmate noted that "[s]ome youths targeted for enslavement found instant sanctuary in joining the Muslims." Billy Wayne Sinclair's account of his Muslim friend, Life, offers an extreme version of how religious values might play a role in gender justice. Active in nurturing new inmates, Life educated inmates on what to expect from prison, and more specifically, on how to protect oneself from victimization. In one episode, after Life hears that a new inmate has been turned out, he becomes enraged and arms himself to confront his attackers. Although another inmate pleads with the men not to "kill each other over an asshole," a fatal battle ensues with Life losing his own life because of "what he believed in—the simple principle that a young man had a right to be free of homosexual slavery."

Life demonstrates how Islam can be a force against violence and homosexuality, but that is not to say that beliefs associated with religion are gender-free. Many of the beliefs espouse a radically hetero-normative worldview that condemns all sex whose aim is not reproductive. Sometimes, the beliefs reinforce other types of gender norms, as Life's instructions about the appropriate response to unwanted advances: "[y]ou get a knife, a ball bat, or a piece of pipe and kill the motherfucker. You hit him and you keep on hitting him till he's dead. When a brother tries to deny a brother the right to be a man, he no longer deserves to live." More extreme, religion may operate as part of an elaborate system of self-identification that undermines reform. For instance, "Prison Islam" or "Prislam" groups model themselves on gang structures and use religious rhetoric to legitimize violence and other criminal activities. Under such ideology, depending on how closely the groups embrace gang culture, it might not be far-fetched to suggest that some Prislam groups are likely to involve themselves in other activities, like gang-rape. Like any intervention effort, the force of religion may have drawbacks in addition to benefits, but it may be that the benefits of more inmates acting like Life still outweigh the costs.

Academics and activists may also have a cultural role in combating gender violence. Accordingly, one scholar suggests that research on prison rape should "draw more upon the vast research on rape in the community," which has been largely neglected "on the assumption that rape in prison is somehow drastically different from the rape of women in the community"; instead there may be deeper links between the two, and an exploration of these similarities might help prison officials reduce the problem. Moreover, PREA-funded studies like *The Myth of Prison Rape* must not go unchallenged by scholars because shoddy work not only is harmful to prisoners, but to scholarship itself.

Art and other forms of cultural productions may be one way of reforming gender consciousness. Despite the difficulty of measuring its impact, some have argued that the arts are an "effective means of intervention for gang-involved and affiliated youth and their families," and that "arts are the best path for change, peace, wholeness, and abundance." In the same way comedians like Jon Stewart and others reinforce negative gender norms, others might use comedy and other social outlets to challenge negative stereotypes. This might include stigmatizing sexual violence in the same way use of crack was culturally shunned and "crack head" became a derogatory epithet; perhaps it is time for rapists and assaulters to bear the brunt of cultural assault. As an illustration, the animated series, Boondocks, constantly discusses the negative effects of prisons and jails, paying critical attention to prison rape. This program puts a comical spin on a subject that is anything but humorous, resulting in a relentless awareness that things are terribly wrong in some prisons. Media outlets are effective at influencing public opinion, and their power may be harnessed to move the issue in a positive direction. This might resonate especially well with the subset of our population that, rather than read esteemed law and policy journals, listens to music, surfs the internet or watches television. Cultural productions like pornography might perpetuate destructive masculinities, but because true arts are about creating, they can be employed to construct new masculinities based on something other than degrading women.

Part III

Islam and U.S. Prisons

"I hereby sentence you to 25 years imprisonment...plenty of time for you to lift weights and convert to Islam." This punch line from a judge in a Chappelle Show comedy skit makes a serious point to introduce the next chapters: Islam holds powerful influence in American prisons. Yet even with an estimated 40,000 prisoners converting to Islam annually in federal and state prisons, there is still scant research on the nature of religion in prison, and to date there are few books that focus on Muslim conversion. What follows helps to fill a critical gap in the study of religion and law, and more specifically, Islam in the correctional setting.

Islam's role in American prisons is part legend, part reality. The Muslim presence in prison is indebted to Muslim outreach efforts that stretch back to Malcolm X's conversion in the 1950s. His story revealed how preaching could facilitate genuine conversion behind bars. For prisons, in general, Islam is a positive force, and for the administration, religious services offer inmates additional ways to channel their time and to try to avoid the subcultures of deviance.

The sequence of the chapters examines conversion from the theoretical to the practical. The first explores prison as a form of "sacred space" or a sanctified space that earns its special position by playing witness to an individual's conversion experiences. This frame allows the reader to consider how a debased and degraded place like prison can become Mecca for a prisoner. The next chapter moves from the micro to the macro to consider patterns of Muslim conversion more broadly. Prison and hip hop culture are important factors for the spread of Islam in America, which has produced a unique feature of conversion to Islam. As countless case studies reveal, African-American converts often undergo two conversions in Islam. The first is due to outreach efforts of radical, race-based traditions of Islam, which are eventually abandoned for a more traditional variety of the faith. In this "double" conversion, Raza Islamica is a concept developed to describe how individuals may abandon a religious organization or ideology, but they never let go of Islam. Instead, they find a different place for themselves under the broad umbrella of the faith. Laying this theoretical groundwork also provides for the reader a sense of the difference between genuine conversion and the process known as radicalization, which is the subject of the following chapter. Although there has been some fervor that prisons are hotbeds of radicalism, such claims have been debunked as overblown, and instead, religion in prison has proved an ally for supporting the process of rehabilitation. The final chapter examines Muslim attitudes toward prisons as expressed by Muslim hip hop artists. For decades Muslim artists have been fierce critics of the criminal justice system, with special misgivings against police and prisons. This part explores the intersection of Islam and American prisons and important issues related to conversion, radicalization, and rehabilitation of inmates.

Chapter 8

God Behind Bars: Race, Religion & Revenge

The U.S. penitentiary is a locus of extreme violence, repression, and control. Its operations are based on a scopic system that subjects detainees to intense and constant surveillance over every inch of the body. This violence is compounded by fights, rapes, beatings, and bodily deprivations that constitute prison life and the lived experiences of prisoners. This volatile atmosphere is organized and structured by the everyday reality of detention and other forms of "legitimate force," the sanctioned violence and punishments inflicted by the state or its agents. Yet within the heart of such savage confines, something quite remarkable takes place. In these debilitating and dehumanizing conditions, religious conversion thrives, and for some, the prison becomes a sanctuary that houses this dramatic and sometimes traumatic transformation. This wretched and filthy place becomes a special, spiritual space—a meta-zone that memorializes and commemorates spiritual rebirth, hierophany, or mysterium tremendum for the ecstatic, emotional, and earth-shaking epiphanies of religious experience. This interaction with the Divine is a rite of passage, which is often predicated on intense emotional feelings of terror and fear; elements that help catalyze the prisoner into a self-governing subject—into a new identity.

This chapter examines the prison as a sacred space. In conversion to Islam, the prison often serves as a sphere of sacrality that facilitates the merger of prisoner and faith. The penitentiary is the subject-forming backdrop for experiences infused with realities of race and religion, creating new spiritual identities within structures of violence. Accordingly, from the early movements of the Moorish Science Temple, Nation of Islam (NOI), and other American Islamic groups, to more contemporary movements like Five Percent Nation and the so-called Latino/Hispanic populations, these new and ever-evolving identities are laced with racial themes and violent motifs.

PRISON IS THE PLACE

The above ideas help to provide some theoretical sketches for analyzing the prison as sacred space. For some behind bars, the prison becomes a site of religious and cultural conversion, and like the prisoner, the prison also converts. As alliances and allegiances are reconfigured in accordance with newfound faith, conceptions of the prison likewise undergo radical revisions. The penal place of "corrections" is reconceived as dar al islam, or a territory guided by Islamic scripture and eschatology. Under the sway of conversion, the world is viewed through the lens of shariah or hadith, and the Islamic community in prison manifests as umma, a holy community of believers, albeit one on lockdown. In this positional paradox, the profane is purified as the filthiest and most forgotten place in America be- comes another's Mecca. In the words of one Muslim convert: "That was a turning point in my life . . . and I don't regret . . . going and experiencing some of the things I experienced . . . in that confinement, or in that restricted area; because in that area I became a man. . . and a free man."

RACE IN PLACE

Under such conditions, it is no surprise that transformations catalyzed by religious conversion are infused by notions of color and race. Since the early 1900s, Islam has played an increasingly important role in the U.S. penitentiary, and most influentially among Black prisoners. For the Black American population, the prisoner-turned-Muslim is a well-known story, firmly etched in cultural memory; a legacy that has been documented in the celebrated Autobiography of Malcolm X (1965), in which three chapters are devoted to Malcolm X's conversion to Islam behind bars. In this story the penitentiary is portrayed as a salvific space that fosters Malcolm X's rehabilitation from "Satan" to "Saved" to "Savior." Describing his initial turn toward Islam, he recounts that "months passed without my even thinking about being imprisoned. In fact, up to then, I never had been so truly free in my life." In another passage, Malcolm X describes his intense shame at not being able to kneel for prayer. He writes: "I had to force myself to bend my knees. And waves of shame and embarrassment would force me back up . . . For the next years, I was the nearest thing to a hermit in the Norfolk Prison Colony. I never have been more busy in my life. I still marvel at how swiftly my previous life's thinking pattern slid away from me, like snow off a roof. It is as though someone else I knew of had lived by hustling and crime. I would be startled to catch myself thinking in a remote way of my earlier self as another person."

ISLAM ON ITS KNEES

Whether relayed by government statistics, academic studies, or by the media, stories about the prison system emphasize violence and disorder. From beatings, stabbings, and killings to legalized state executions, the life of a prisoner is portrayed as brutal. Constant surveillance is backed by the full power of modern technology, which results in a new and improved panoptical field. The effects of such penal voyeurism can be so tremendous that in its perfected application, the prisoner becomes his own guard, or as Michel Foucault explains, "he inscribes in himself the power relation in which he simultaneously plays both roles; he becomes the principle of his own subjection." The impact of this tense environment on religious life is no exception, and so Islamic practice must adapt to these conditions, or be abandoned altogether.

CONCLUSION

I have argued that the penitentiary plays a central role in the identity, memory, and religiosity of many Muslims and Muslim converts. For both, "place" brands itself onto individual and collective religious memory, and sacred space serves as a metaphysical gate-way—a mundane area that becomes a sanctuary. For converts, the prison's visual, physical, and mental systems of control are relegated to a second order and replaced by a new regime: self-control. The subject-forming space that facilitates this transition becomes forever branded onto the believer's religious imagination, infused with the everyday violence of the institution. This newly discovered self-empowerment, though defiantly distant from the repenter envisioned by the penitentiary's original framers, is nonetheless a reality of today's prisons. Such happenings behind prison walls, in turn, become immortalized through cultural production and reproduction, and for many Black Muslims, the enslavement in Egypt, America, and now in American prisons, all weave together into narratives of persecution and domination imposed on dark-skinned Muslims and their spiritual ancestors. As Malcolm X put it: "America is facing judgment just like Egypt was judged for enslaving the Hebrews, and Babylon was judged for enslaving the Hebrews. . . Today America is faced with the same thing . . . and will be destroyed as surely as Egypt was destroyed and Babylon was destroyed." This creative imagery and rhetorical resistance all point to a future where righteousness is unveiled and the captives are set free—*are literally set free.*

Chapter 9

Raza Islamica: Prisons, Hip Hop & Converting Converts

A lot of rules, some locked in solitude
Curse the day of they birth confused, who's to be praised?
The mighty dolla or almighty Allah?
—Nas from *Ghetto Prisoners*

I. INTRODUCTION

Hip hop culture's very birth in the United States coincided with an incarceration explosion in the 1970s that persists to the present. The rebirth of the prison would become an ever-present menace to the hip hop generation, which would feel the first-hand effects of losing someone to the prisons. This trend in growth would go on to make the U.S. prison population the largest in the globe—a multi-billion dollar industry with two million inmates and counting—at roughly the same time hip hop grew into a multi-billion dollar industry of its own. The growth of prisons and hip hop culture was both coterminous and coextensive.

The lengthy history shared by American Muslim movements and U.S. prisons was notable by the 1920s, when prison outreach efforts were well underway. Malcolm X's prison conversion took place in the 1950s, however, before him Elijah Muhammad, the founder of the Nation of Islam (NOI), had spent time incarcerated. Muhammad's spiritual predecessor W. D. Fard also had a case file with the FBI and was arrested several times. Similarly, Five Percent Nation of Islam founder, Clarence 13X, was incarcerated for two years. Thus, the study of Islam in the United States will likely simultaneously lead to the examination of the country's jails, prisons, and other institutions of confinement. One cannot examine Islam in America without examining the interconnectivity and self-discovery of oppressed and confined people, and Islam's unique historical significance in both pan-African and Latino contexts.

General Trends in Growth

Prisons and hip hop music are conduits for the spread of Islam in the United States. Despite the varying numbers, scholars, chaplains, and some prison officials claim that Islam is the fastest growing religion behind bars. Although there are no reliable statistics compiled for the number of Muslim prisoners in all American institutions of imprisonment, it has been estimated that nationwide, fifteen-percent of the U.S. prison population is Muslim. Elsewhere, this estimate has been quantified to be as roughly as 300,000 and 350,000. At the federal level, the Office of the Inspector General reports that approximately six percent of the 150,000 federal inmates seek Islamic services. Asma Gull Hasan in 1991 estimated that 35,000 prisoners annually converted to Islam, and more recent estimates put conversions to Islam in all city, state, and federal institutions annually at 30,000 or 40,000. These figures suggest that there have been some 300,000 conversions in prison within the last decade, the majority of which are by African-Americans.

Fertile Fields: Mass Incarceration & Hip Hop Culture

Islam's success in prison is matched only by its influence on hip hop culture, and there are complex mappings among all three cultures. In the way Islam is dubbed the "official religion" of hip hop, one might describe rap as the "official music" of the penitentiary. In turn, rap's discursive focus on the prison may have much to do with the NOI, which has "greatly impacted the [hip hop nation]." Rap's influence on prison culture goes hand-in-hand with prisons possessing gang populations.

For some who turn to Islam in prison, a foundation for conversion was likely set long before they entered the prison gates, given the closeness and brotherhood found in gangs, which Islam further fosters. As Robert Dannin explains, "[d]octrinally correct or not, the gangstas have been 'dropping' Islamic symbols for decades and setting the table for genuine conversion once the adolescent's moratorium becomes a serious quest for meaning and values." Even if this religious orientation is not evident to the listener at the time, Walker explains that "motifs from Islam have increasingly tinged general African-American rap culture with which new generations of non-Muslim teenagers are growing up—setting up a context for later conversion . . . ."

II. FAITH IN PRISONS, MUSIC

Rap's first major reference to the prison system came in the 1982 release of Grand Master Flash's *The Message*, which in achieving critical acclaim, reached a milestone for rap music. The title track has been described as "one of the most important songs in hip hop history," and its scathing critique on American society forever linked the brutal realities of prison life with the hip hop generation:

> Turned stickup kid, look what you done did Got sent up for a eight year bid
> Now your manhood is took and you're a may tag Spend the next two years as an undercover fag Being used and abused and served like hell. Till one day you was found hung dead in a cell It was plain to see that your life was lost. You was cold as your body swung back and forth But now your eyes sing the sad, sad song. Of how you lived so fast and died so young...

Yet, this unblinking commentary on life in the ghetto did not develop in a vacuum: the Furious Five were certainly influenced by Islamic teachings and at the very least, one member, "Rahiem," was a member of the Five Percent Nation. This orientation jibes with a flyer from 1980 that advertised "The Grandmaster Flash Show" starring "Allah Sounds" while others in the hip hop scene mixed in Islamic themes, including "DJ Islam," whose namesake would be joined by the up-and- coming producer Afrika Islam and rapper T.C. Islam. From its seedling days, hip hop culture began to represent itself with Islamic names, themes, and symbols.

Like their poetical predecessors Public Enemy, the self-styled "prophets of rage," later generations of rap artists see themselves as messiahs or ones chosen to lead the people. Brother Ali's "Pickett Fence" describes how, at an early age, he discovered his special relationship with God:

> "You look the way you do because you're special Not the short bus way, I mean that God's gonna test you And all of this pain is training for the day when you will have to lead with the gift God gave to you Grown folks don't see it but the babies do And there's a chance that you can save a few."

III. ISLAM INCARCERATED:RELIGION AS REHABILITATION

> *Collect calls to the till, sayin' how ya changed Oh you a Muslim now, no more dope game; heard you might be comin' home, just got bail Wanna go to the Mosque, don't wanna chase tail. It seems I lost my little homie he's a changed man Hit the pen and now no sinnin' is the game plan*
>
> —Tupac Shakur from
> *I Ain't Mad at Cha*

Penal trends in the United States depict a system that has largely given up on the idea of inmate rehabilitation. Despite this revised political posture, religion certainly has not given up on inmate rehabilitation. One study noted that the practice of religion "in prison can be very extensive with about 50% of inmates attending religious services an average of six times per month." Moreover, large and supermax prison inmates see the coming and going of priests, imams, and other clerical figures who contribute to the wide array of religious services held by, among others, members of Christian, Islamic, Jewish, and Native-American faiths. As houses of penitence, penitentiaries have historically provided the space for spiritual transformation, including the famous "born-again" Christian. Today is no different, and conversion is alive and thriving, except that nowadays Islam is the religion of choice, making prisons "a major recruiting ground for Islam." Prisons are "major centers of Muslim reflection and identity," and the Muslim prison ministry uses these centers to penetrate nominal Christians. *The Encyclopedia of Prisons and Correctional Facilities* (2005) noted that ninety percent of more than one hundred African-American masjids are

SpearIt

actively involved in prison ministries and ministries to ex-offenders, while some provide temporary shelter for those released from prison.

In general, religion is associated with positive effects on offenders, and research indicates that high levels of participation in religious activities can reduce juvenile delinquency. In adult prisons, religious involvement can reduce prisoner misconduct and is reported as a viable correctional intervention. In a study on the attributes of those who escaped recidivism, religious transformation is one of the primary themes. The Department of Human Health and Services reports that the existing "body of literature is consistent with criminological theories, supporting the claim that religious beliefs are inversely related to delinquency, crime, and recidivism."

Islam's success in reforming inmates may relate structurally to the original intent of the penitentiary, or as D.C. Corrections chaplain Imam Mikal Huda Ba'th explains, "[a] cursory review of the acknowledged intentions of Islam and the Quaker reformists shows that it is apparent the objective of both religious ideologies is to instill penitence in the criminal." Furthermore, Dannin notes that "low recidivism rates and success in the rehabilitation of drug and alcohol addiction win tolerance, even approval, for Muslims," a point that echoes Lincoln's pioneering study that notes how recovering alcoholics and addicts were able to cope more effectively after converting to Islam. These indications support the Department of Human Health's positive assessment of "how religious programming may be uniquely suited to both facilitate and augment the ongoing process of prisoner reentry."

But why do inmates convert to Islam specifically? To begin, many Muslims believe that conversion to Islam is really a "reversion," since every human being is born a Muslim already. Others subscribe to the ideology due to Islamic history in Africa, which offers an opportunity to embrace a long lost identity. In James' analysis, conversion often attends sudden events or trying circumstances, a point that may connect to conversion's prevalence in the penitentiary. Malcolm X, likewise, typifies this notion when he writes of the traumas of solitary confinement that precluded his conversion. Recent accounts of conditions in federal prisons, Abu-Ghraib, and Guantanamo Bay seemingly attest that such brutal and terrifying conditions of imprisonment persist. The traumatizing episodes of the prison experience may help set the conditions that make inmates ripe for religious conversion. The crisis of solitary confinement alone can catalyze a quest for meaning that moves beyond the bars. This view of conversion is akin to a deprivation perspective, where loss of liberty, goods, services, sexual relations, and security inspire the quest for meaning in the correctional environment.

The stress of prison life is a major factor and, "for some inmates religion is one of their methods of coping because it offers them a variety of ways to help endure the stressors often associated with the prison environment." Writing on the motivations of radical conversion, Alison Pargeter identifies "acute personal crisis and in some cases mental breakdowns" as motivating factors for conversion.

IV. CONCLUSIONS: FACING A NEW DIRECTION

> *The color-blindness of the Muslim world's religious society and the color-blindness of the Muslim world's human society: these two influences have each day been making a greater impact, and an increasing persuasion against my previous way of thinking.*
>
> --Malcolm X from the
> *Autobiography of Malcolm X*

The available research on conversion to Islam in America features a significant and repetitive story: how quickly each individual makes it on the path will vary, but the steps are generally the same. The initial turn to Islam often starts with groups which many Muslims would deny as authentic. It is a journey that begins with movements and organizations that are considered at least unorthodox, if not fully heretical from the mainstream point of view. In due time, however, the convert engages in another bout of soul-searching and moves beyond the racial trappings to embrace every Muslim, no matter the skin color. In the transition to mainstream Islam, just how many adopt Sunni, Shia, or Sufi forms, in particular, awaits further study.

Such testimony points to a process by which the marginal movements of Islam are hard at work in the service of the mainstream, priming their converts for the second conversion to Islam. That is, many who join these groups eventually seek to become a part of the broader Islamic world, which causes them to abandon an ideology, *but they never abandon Islam*. Instead, orthodox African-American Muslims often go through two conversions in their Muslim spiritual lives. Thus, as the Muslim population continues to grow in the United States, it must be recognized that this is partially due to organizations like the NOI and the Five Percent, groups which have brought many to Islam, even if to a "watered-down" version, eventually leading these believers to join the ranks of *Raza Islamica*.

Chapter 10

Muslim Radicalization in Prison: Responding with Sound Penal Policy or the Sound of Alarm?

I.   APPROACHING AND INTERPRETING PRISONER RADICALIZATION

"Radicalization," according to one inmate, is when "prisons try to promote Christianity and starve Islam." This statement came in a letter from a Muslim inmate, Abdullah al-Muhajair, sent to Representative Peter King in his role as chair of the 2011 U.S. congressional hearings entitled, *The Threat of Muslim- American Radicalization in U.S. Prisons.* Representative King's opinion on this matter sees Islamic radicalization as a unique threat since Muslims are, as he claims, "the only group in prison which is tied to overseas terrorists which is part of an existential threat to the United States." Hence, his account of the problem sits diametrically opposed to al-Muhajair's views, which together underscore the critical need to approach the question of prisoner radicalization with a sense of caution and consistency.

What follows relies on ethnographic sources to explore radicalization among Muslim prisoners. The data sets include testimony from incarcerated Muslims, testimony from congressional hearings, and case studies involving Muslim inmates and extremist violence. The data is examined in light of recent research on administrative and penal policies in prison. Together these sources reveal the complex relationship between the prison environment and radicalization.

This chapter starts with a simple question: What exactly is *radicalization*? To be certain, the term is a very recent creation, gaining widespread use in the years following the attacks of 9/11 and becoming intertwined with the Muslim faith. In broad strokes, the term indicates a process or means by which one adopts *radicalism* or *radical* beliefs and behaviors. This much is simple, but determining the exact content of *radical* is not always certain since the term has historically attached to different meanings. For example, early use of radical was loyal to the etymology of *rad*, which meant "radish" or "roots," hence, a radical connoted one returning to "roots" of tradition—the origins or essence.

Used this way, radical overlaps in meaning with the notion of *fundamentalist*, which similarly conveys a turn to the basics or fundamentals. Later use of radical, however, would connote a somewhat opposite meaning, as movement away from a particular norm, being "far out" or "extreme" with respect to the cultural status quo. Such use is not typically viewed as a pejorative since radicals were often seen as progressives who contributed to the development of thought, politics, and culture.

Today, however, the meaning of radicalization is not typically intended as a positive association. More particularly, it has been something of a code for violent behavior and ideology, despite the fact that violence is the exception among radicals. Take, for example, 2006 congressional hearings, where one expert testified: "Occasionally, I am asked to describe the typical radicalized inmate. While it seems a reasonable question, I would suggest that focusing only on individual inmates is not an appropriate solution. In fact, *terrorism* is a team sport." This perspective corroborates with the New York City Police Department's model of radicalization, which concludes at a stage of violence called "jihadization." More formal attempts to define radicalization follow suit, including the Department of Justice's definition as "the process by which inmates who do not invite or plan overt terrorist acts adopt extreme views, including beliefs that violent measures need to be taken for political or religious purposes." Characterized as such, radicalization is hardly a principled concept, and instead functions as a catchall for "what goes on before the bomb goes off." The ascriptions are typically couched in terms of good and bad, right and wrong, and other dichotomies that convey the subjective perceptions of physical danger.

The logic is flawed; radicalization is an insufficient cause of terrorism, most obviously because most radicals are not terrorists. Indeed extremism cuts both ways, and just as one can will toward extremist violence, another can toward extreme pacifism. Individuals like Mahatma Gandhi and Martin Luther King were radicals of the first order, bent on non-violence at all costs. Yet this dimension of radicalization is lost in today's usage. Unfortunately, violence-based logic leads to fallacious forms of debate in which radicalization is viewed as the root cause of terrorism and, in turn, terrorism is proof of one's radicalization. Yet radicalism itself is an insufficient predictor of terrorism, since most extremists do not engage in violent activities. This point is supported by more recent creations of phrases like *violent radicalization* or *militant radicalization*, to indicate a difference between radical thought and violent behavior. As one study admonishes:

Radicalization should not be viewed as an escalator, inevitably carrying all the individuals on it inexorably into violence. It is better envisaged as a funnel that large number of individuals may enter but from which only a very small number of individuals emerge. Many will drop out along the way, leaving only a small proportion to cross the Rubicon and become involved in terrorism.

In this crossing, there is no singular pathway to becoming radical, and no single factor for adopting extremist views.

II.   ALARMISM AND POLITICAL DISTORTIONS

It is critical to understand how fear-based perceptions about Muslims and Islam have hampered objective inquiry into Islam in prison, and perhaps more critically, how they have concretely informed penal policy. Despite three congressional hearings and a growing body of scholarly research, there are still many unknowns. More certain, however, is that perceptions about Islam in prison are tainted by a climate of suspicion and fear, some of which derive from fears entirely unrelated to Islam, including multiple perceived threats—criminals, prisoners, gang members, African-Americans, Latinos, and Muslims—a mix that can easily overflow into unthinking hysteria.

Despite many uncertainties about radicalization as a phenomenon, politicians and other state officials have not refrained from making overreaching claims about radicalization and prisons. To illustrate, during the 2006 U.S. Senate hearings on prisoner radicalization, Senator Jon Kyl (Arizona, Republican) asserted, "Jose Padilla, a terrorist accused of trying to build a dirty bomb to unleash in the United States was exposed to radical Islam in the U.S. prison." In the 2011 hearings, experts and politicians alike continued to invoke Jose Padilla as an inmate who was radicalized in prison. Even prior to the 2011 hearings, Republican staffers for the Committee on Homeland Security distributed a background sheet entitled *Background Information on Prominent Post-9/11 U.S. Prison Radicalization Cases*, which listed Padilla as a prison convert. However, Padilla did not convert to Islam until *after* he was released, nor did he travel to Afghanistan and Pakistan until seven years *after* his parole.

The same information sheet lists other inaccurate information. It describes James Cromitie as being "radicalized in prison," despite the fact that he was paroled in 2004 and was not arrested on terror-related crimes until five years later. Despite the use of him and others as poster boys for inmate radicalization, there is little evidence, either before or immediately after their incarceration, to connect time in prison causally to acts of violent extremism. The sheet also cites Michael Finton as "radicalized in an Illinois state prison," without evidence to substantiate the claim; similarly, it cites the Lackawanna Six terror plot without any explanation of why this case counts as prison radicalization. Furthermore, it cites to the abovementioned 2010 report, overseen by Senator John Kerry (Massachusetts, Democrat), which described three dozen prison converts who went to Yemen to learn Arabic. Careful scrutiny of the report raises serious doubts that this should be a part of the information sheet. The report states, "U.S. officials told [c]ommittee staff that they *fear* that these Americans were radicalized in prison and traveled to Yemen for training." These statements came with no citations for the statements, no evidence of the extremism or intent to commit violence, and no mention of who the prisoners were; and the beliefs about radicalization were admittedly based on fear. Although this report contained no verifiable evidence that these individuals had converted, much less were radicalized in prison, the story was accepted and invoked as evidence throughout the rest of the report.

Like Padilla, commentators repeatedly cite Richard Reid, the shoe bomber, as an example of prisoner radicalization. Although scholarly works, think-tank publications, and congressional statements and reports cite his name, there is little to support the claim that he was radicalized in prison. In fact, a closer look at the historical record suggests that he likely adopted extremist beliefs, and sought to engage in violence after he spent time at the Brixton mosque where he regularly heard sermons from the Abdullah El-Faisal, who was arrested in 2003 for attempting to incite violence.

As these cases indicate, inaccuracy and misinformation plague inquiry into Muslim-American prisoners. These and other challenges surmount the quest to understand extremism in prison beyond the idea that Muslims are a particularly deadly threat.

III.   MUSLIMS IN CRIMINAL JUSTICE

This part explores Islam's legacy in U.S. courts and prisons. For well over half a century, Muslims have used courts to establish religious rights for inmates in the same time Islamic outreach groups were assisting inmates through prison ministry and re-entry support. This history of Islam in prisons offers a compelling counter-narrative to the distortions described above.

Penal and Cultural Impacts

Like the impact Muslims have had on prison law, the practical impact of the religion on the lives of inmates and prison culture is unmistakable. The religion offers a set of practices and doctrines for inmates, including the proclamation of faith, prayer, charity, and fasting, among other traditional and non-traditional pieties. These practices help develop discipline and structure in individuals whose lives are characterized by chaos and instability, teaching selflessness in a world of self-interest. In turn, inmates refer to Islam through many images, including as a "lifeboat" that saved a life, or as a "sword" that cuts through "ignorance and repression," "eye drops for those with irritated eyes." One Latino convert at Folsom State Prison in California explained Islam's meaning for prisoners: "For those that are serious and involved in the greater Jihad (Struggle of Self), Islam is an anchor to a world that is lost to us behind these cement walls and iron bars. It offers love and hope, and most of all, peace that comes when one surrenders to Allah."

It is not uncommon for inmates to interpret and understand their imprisonment within an Islamic framework. This is possible due to the fact that prisons and penance both have a place in Islam. As one Muslim chaplain notes, "A cursory review of the acknowledged intentions of Islam and the Quaker reformists shows that it is apparent the objective of both religious ideologies is to instill penitence in the criminal." One scholar notes prisons were not unfamiliar in the Quran, and are mentioned at least nine times as an institution. In the centuries following the founding of Islam, prisons would become more widely used within Islamic governance. Called "*nafi'a*," or "beneficent," the goal of punishment was intended to "benefit" the prisoner. Hence, there is considerable overlap with this concept and "penance," which informed the creation of penitentiaries in European Catholic traditions and later Protestant varieties in the United States. Just how many inmates make these connections is uncertain, but some inmates recognize the importance of imprisonment in religious narrative, as one African-American convert from San Quentin State Prison writes, "We must retain in mind that nearly all of the primordial Imams of Ahl Al-Bayt (the household of the Prophet) were imprisoned or under house arrest by the prevailing anti-Hashimite authorities of the time."

Islam's practical value in prison links to a strong emphasis on communal worship and diversity of denominations. Islam offers inmates something different from what Christian reformers envisioned in cloistered reflection or silent prayer. The practices are better suited for building social networks, and as one scholar asserts, "The greater the capacity of the prison jamaat to establish the privilege of congregational prayer, the greater the potential effect on the Muslim." The communal worship, egalitarianism, and positive identity construction all serve to support moral and social discipline in inmates, upholding Quran institutions, encouraging a rigorous program of study and prayer, and offering a "counter disciplinary resistance" to the hierarchies that define prison culture. For some, it offers a regime to resist American culture in general, particularly "Black Muslim" organizations, which have effectively captured the attention of those who have experienced racial oppression. For others who fall into Sunni circles, there is a very different effect of faith, and there is scriptural emphasis on equality and belief in God and righteous conduct, not skin color, nationality or political creed. This practical orientation, which supports ties both inside and outside prison, is cited as particularly suited for individuals in an environment where racial tensions run high. Still for others whose piety flows to Sufi forms of the tradition, inmates whose lives are laced with violence cultivate pacifism and non-violent principles. Taken wholly, the results are significant, according to one Muslim inmate at the Stafford Creek Corrections Center in Washington state, who describes the long-term effects of commitment to Islam as "wholly positive and liberating despite the anti-Islam rhetoric we hear so much of in the West."

According to such testimony, Islamic values and mores converge with desired penal outcomes on multiple levels, including conversion itself. As a process that involves turning away from previous aspects of one's life, for some, conversion represents the shedding of one's identification as a criminal or gang member. As one inmate from Pelican Bay State Prison described, "I have seen people who were so confused about their present situation (incarceration) that they would victimize each other. But . . . many of them have rehabilitated themselves. These men are now ready to be placed back on the street to keep another generation from coming into prisons."

Sometimes an inmate's conversion to Islam impacts the very inmates who witness the transformation. According to veteran prison-preacher Imam Muhammad Abdullah of Taif Tul Islam in Los Angeles, when other prisoners witness the transformative impact of a conversion, this has profound consequences on those inmates: "[T]he discipline that Islam requires and cleanliness, are really admired by people . . . this begins a conversion of many because they are either living with their former crime partner(s) and they knew his or their past and to see that person or people change right before their very eyes is enough for anyone to see there must be a just god." Research supports that such transformations have a strong impact on others, as one study noted, "When people say that they feel peace or that they have found freedom within their imprisonment, any listener cannot help but be swayed by the obvious emotion with which they speak."

Although there is need for further research on Islam's influences on inmates, the available scholarship points to positive links between Islam and inmate rehabilitation. Given how Islam connects inmates to their African and African-American heritage, it is hardly cultural apostasy for African-Americans to convert to Islam, since doing so takes them to the very heart of Africa. As one African-American inmate describes, "Islam encourages togetherness, prayer, and aspects of morality that would, literally, awe the average Westerner. Islam encourages family adhesiveness and history . . . and gave me the encouragement to identify with Africa."

Latinos adopt a similar cultural logic and embrace Islam as a way of reconnecting to their Spanish heritage. Although data on Latino conversion is sparse, and even less is known about conversion in prison, some studies confirm its occurrence. For Latinos, the draw of Islam is perhaps unlike that of any other religion due to historical factors similar to those that define the African-American experience. As the term "Moor" was embraced by various African-American leaders to unite the poor and disenfranchised with Islam, the Latino embrace of Moorish Spain provides a powerful tool to re-imagine identity. As one Mexican-American convert from Huntsville Unit, a prison in Texas, described: "When I learned 'ojala' (God willing) was from Arabic, I saw the truth about Hispanics and Islam. I've heard my parents say that a thousand times, but never really thought about it. Now I know and tell others that Mexicans got Islam in their blood."

Highlighting the positive impacts of embracing Islam inside prison walls, however, should not ignore certain negative outcomes. For example, as one African-American convert describes, "There are no incentives (worldly) to embracing Islam in the prison system, especially since the aftermath of Sept. 11th, and subsequent events which only cast a negative image upon Islam, but have led the U.S. government to view Muslim prisoners as potential terrorists." Yet, the hardships that may be involved with accepting Islam does not stop inmates from converting. The consequences have their own set of ramifications, including having to live with the adverse effects. For example, one African-American convert asserts, "In the bible belt families have been known to disown their loved ones inside because they embrace Islam." Writing from Union Correctional Institute in Florida, he describes, "[W]ith all the negative which comes with prisoners embracing Islam, they continue to come to Islam at a steady pace, knowing that it will likely only make their time harder."

Other adverse consequences of accepting Islam run along ethnic lines, and inmates who convert are at risk from members of their own ethnic group. As indicated by one Native-American convert from Corcoran State Prison, "When a non-African-American accepts Islam such as myself, I opened up a very dangerous door that could lead to physical and verbal abuse bye [sic] fellow Native-Americans because I accepted Islam." His troubles resound with those expressed by a Latino ex-prisoner who himself was not Muslim, but described seeing a Latino convert to Islam who was "dealt with in a horrible way." As these individuals convey, embracing Islam comes with a price tag, sometimes even violence. The overarching conclusion suggests the benefits of Islam outweigh the harms and negatives associated with becoming Muslim.

It is impossible to deny that protection-based motives cause some prisoners to turn to Islam. One inmate explains that offering protection is simply a part of being in a Muslim brotherhood: "Some brothers were born Muslim, and chose the street life over Muslim life only to return to it once entering the system, because with the Muslims there is a sense of structure, order, purpose, and some just seek a sense of protection, which is what we are here for." Sometimes a person who enters Islam out of self-interest will end up keeping the faith, as one inmate who converted in a Los Angeles County jail describes: "Although I entered Islam with an ulterior motive, my heart was already open to God and Allah is slowly but surely purifying my mind and spirit." His words suggest that even if an inmate joins Islam for physical protection, it is no barrier to developing faith. However, such motivations should not be exaggerated, as one ex-gang member writes from prison, "These days when asked if one became Muslim for protection, the retort is 'yes, for Allah's protection!'"

At present, little is known about Islam's impact on gang culture, and little is mentioned in social science studies about the influence of religion in a youth's ability to leave a gang. One researcher has suggested that religion functions similarly "to gang affiliation and the need to connect to other people." Despite the gap in research, it is clear that many who are now law-abiding Muslims were once gang members, as detailed by one African-American prisoner who writes, "When an individual wants to leave the gang life, most likely he enters into this community. He knows that we will support him and assist him put his life in order. It is not unusual to see gang members become ex-gang members." The turn from gangs is complex, yet as another inmate attests, "I believe the fact that young men in gangs are often primed for Islam as a result of the hardships they endure in their youth. Once in prison they are under no illusion about the American Dream . . . . Most young men in gangs come from impoverished homes with enormous voids in their lives and Islam brings substance to their lives." Unfortunately, however, as the next section shows, in prison this is not always the message spread in the name of Islam.

IV. RADICALIZATION IN PRISON

The Fertile Soil of Jihad?

Focusing on the prison population, evidence shows the number of cases in which an inmate or recent inmate was involved in terrorist activity is extremely small. In the global context, one study identified forty-six cases out of tens of thousands of terrorist attacks in which a stretch in prison contributed to a radicalization process, leading eventually to a terrorist attack or threat against Western targets between 1968 and 2009. In the United States, there has been little terrorist activity involving Muslim inmates. According to a Congressional Research Service (CRS) study, of fifty-three identified terror plots of "[h]omegrown *violent* jihadist activity," only one case, the JIS, definitively involved violent extremism that was connected to a U.S. prison. These statistics have led one commentator to suggest that if prisons are producing terrorists like a factory, they are doing a terrible job. Furthermore, in 2007, the FBI conducted over 2,088 terrorism threat assessments in prisons and jails across the United States and "determined that there was *not* a JIS-like pattern of terrorist recruitment in U.S. prisons . . . . Indeed, the FBI could find no pattern of terrorist recruitment whatsoever."

Prisoner Perceptions

In his letter to Representative King, al-Muhajair illuminates what has propelled him to become an "enemy of the United States": "I will spare you all the reasons, except to mention . . . cowardly bombing of Muslim women and children in a sovereign nation . . . thirty billion a year to Israel in weapons to kill Muslims, genocide of civilians in Iraq, Afghanistan, human rights violations at Gitmo, I am sure you get the point."

Disaffection from government polices abroad and at home is common among Muslim inmates. In al-Muhajair's case, feelings of anger and alienation led him to renounce his citizenship, only to be ignored by the government. He claims to have sent "letter after letter to the INS Dep[artment] of State all in accordance with 8 USCS 1481 (A)(6)." This particular statute affords a citizen the opportunity to renounce citizenship. Yet, al-Muhajair claims that his letters never got a response. He marvels at the government's laxity: "[H]ow is it a right given to me by Congress of the United States can be voided by [a]gency in-action?" More ominously, however, al-Muhajair points to the consequences of his treatment, "Seems the [Department] of [S]tate doesn't know what happens when you corner a badger." His statements offer insight into inmate extremism and suggest there is plenty of fuel for radicalization at home—prison radicals need no proselytizing from foreigners—they are fully capable of radicalizing other inmates on their own. This is obvious in al-Muhajair's letter, which laments, "I don't understand why it is ignored. The holy Quran gives one a choice of fight or flight, why does America want me to fight? I will die for Allah, what land will it be on?"

Criminal Justice Critiques

From the days of Malcolm X to the present, Muslims invoke the criminal justice system as a major source of oppression against the poor, minorities, and Muslims themselves. This tradition continues and inmates hold deep animus from their experiences in criminal justice at all levels—cops, courts, and corrections. Regarding the latter, one Muslim prisoner in California describes the environment itself as causing one to seek survival over all: "Prisons are the only means by which man can legally enslave another man, so it is not difficult to see that there is and are ulterior motives for the crafty to keep men down and willing to do whatever to get ahead in this ruthless environment." Similar invective was expressed by an elderly African-American prisoner who voiced his disdain for the prison system by unfailingly signing all his letters with "Free the oppressed (90:11-13)."

Particular tensions for Muslim prisoners arise from negative interactions with prison guards, particularly in the aftermath of 9/11. In Malcolm X's days, guards were antagonistic to the point of radicalizing inmates as he recalls, "I have heard scores of new prisoners swearing back in their cells that when free their first act would be to waylay those visiting-room guards. Hatred often focused on them." His statement vividly captures the possibility that prison staff and policy can actually stoke inmate radicalization and perhaps, extremist violence as well. The same holds true in the present as expressed by an ex-gang member who cites his own experiences of being placed in solitary confinement. He used a homemade wick as an incense holder, which he was previously allowed. "Observing this quite common occurrence a guard who had previously commented on my religious attire as a 'nightgown' decided that this was some sort of explosive device, and I was subsequently thrown into ad-seg." Another inmate, from Union Correctional Institute in Florida adds, "We are under tremendous pressure and scrutiny due to the War on Terror; guards target Muslim prisoners for harassment, and sometimes, target other black prisoner for no other reason than because they think they are Muslim." Similar sentiment was expressed by an African-American convert who describes his own daydreams of getting even with guards:

> It may seem petty and stupid, but after while it's aggravating and offends the senses when guards just refer to us as "Taliban" or call one of us "Mohammad." Sometimes I catch myself just fantasizing about how to settle the score and get back at them . . . . [T]here is one guard in particular—he hates us and it shows. Like I said it's petty, but I'm just saying what happens.

Finding irony in the treatment of Muslims by guards, one prisoner from California State Prison, Corcoran writes, "They always talk about gangs and Islam as if it's the same thing. But they never once look at how they look with their boots, badges, and shaved heads. That's pot calling kettle 'black.'" Another inmate describes experiences with guards in a California prison: "I have been harassed, discriminated against, ridiculed, falsely accused and wrongly placed in ad-seg by a group of guards . . . . [One guard] openly ridiculed my Islamic clothing." Such treatment leads inmates to other conclusions, like one California convert who writes, "Muslims, in prison, are conscious and the system has declared war on us. Implicit in inmates' views about their treatment at the hands of the justice system is widespread belief that the deck is stacked against criminal defendants. One inmate in California describes the severity of the system at multiple intersections: "I've been incarcerated for 13 years. I received a 20-year sentence for drug trafficking, and am a first-time offender . . . . I've been to six different institutions, and of course have been subjected to discrimination for nothing other than being <u>Muslim</u>, then there's being a <u>convict</u> and being <u>Black</u>." Another Muslim inmate described the U.S. government and the criminal justice system as "accomplices" since, according to him, "All minority prisoners are 'political prisoners' because under the current imprisonment [sic] policies established by politicians and government officials, all imprisonment is substantively political." For others, Islam is a path to recreating one's self by erasing the iniquities brought on by the justice system, as described by one African-American inmate:

> Muslim converts behind bars are those who come from a gang lifestyle and frequent run-ins with police and authorities. And in my opinion, most were subjected to selective justice . . . . [I]f one was arrested and convicted for robbery, he would be given stiffer punishment if he or she were black or Latino. Islam offers these kinds of people a new start. A chance to dump their baggage of hate and malice.

Of the justice system's branches, for Muslims the overwhelming target of dissent is the prison system. The sustained criticism is noteworthy and images are vivid, such as one inmate's account of life for prisoners: "Each and every day, prisoners are subject to brutality, inhumanity and degradation. Sick prisoners are allowed to linger days and nights in pain without help and who eventually die. Prisoners are thrown down stairs while handcuffed . . . . Massive psychological torture, and mental illness uncared for, occurs daily in U.S. prisons." One African-American convert indicates how such experiences were deeply linked to his turn to the faith: "[I've] seen almost every evil that ever could happen within these concentration camp walls, so brotherhood is just not something I've given into. We are being somewhat oppressed . . . these are all crisis [sic] that people of color face daily. Al-Islam is the only answer for men, women, and children." Another inmate in Missouri reiterates the plight for Muslims at his institution: "The Prison Administration here is certainly against us. They do everything in there [sic] power to oppress us."

Racial and Religious Discrimination

Related to their experiences in criminal justice is a sense of general discrimination of Muslims in free society. Al-Muhajair's letter to Representative King cites such oppression as the catalyst for the "Fort Hood shooting": "What do Americans expect, 'Major Malik Nadal?' Work on a base and see every day Muslims being killed (what did you expect??). I think he is a hero and I am sorry he ran out of bullets." Practices of discrimination are sometimes so pervasive that non-Muslims are subject to hostility simply for looking like Muslims, as Representative Al Green described at the 2011 hearings: "I want you to

SpearIt

know that when I board an airplane, I am looked upon with an eye of suspicion. For some reason people tend to think that I am Muslim. For some reason, a person told me I needed to go back home to my foreign country, that I don't belong in this country."

Like the religious discrimination Representative Green relates, inmates commonly cite experiencing racial inequities in American society and prison. This may explain in part why groups like the NOI have been successful in recruiting members—the group speaks to those who experience racism first-hand. For example, Malcolm X's conversion to Islam in prison back in the 1950s was largely based on his attraction to the racial rhetoric, which helped him conclude: "[A]mong all Negroes the black convict is the most perfectly preconditioned to hear the words, 'the white man is the devil.'"

The war on terror is an important symbol of oppression for inmate perceptions. Whether it be the rounding up of Arab-Americans or non-citizens, or torture at the Abu-Ghraib and Guantanamo prisons, inmates know first-hand that the burdens of war are not shouldered equally. The use of "war," both literally and metaphorically, might encourage a war-like mentality. It might be little surprise, then, that extremist inmates understand the situation in like terms, or as al-Muhajair's letter explains, "I am a Muslim, and I feel because of America's 'war on Islam' I am the enemy of the United States." In similar vein, another Muslim inmate adds, "A war is being waged on poor and minority communities across the U.S. The result of all this warfare has been the absolute decimation of our communities, and an ongoing SOCIAL GENOCIDE of people of color. Around the globe we must demand that this social genocide STOP NOW!"

V.   CONCLUSION AND FORWARD

These findings lead to telling conclusions that bear on penal and public policy. Perhaps, the greatest contribution is showing how political responses to prisoner radicalization are misguided, and based on false data and flawed analyses. Although less than a handful of Muslim inmates became involved in terrorist activity in the past decade, the issue has been overblown, perhaps best evidenced by the fact that there were more congressional hearings in the last decade on violent extremism among Muslim inmates than actual instances of it.

The Sound of Sirens

Violent extremism among Muslim inmate populations is relatively rare in the post-9/11 era. This fact is noteworthy for policymakers since it provides an opportunity to reconsider assumptions and perceptions about Islam in prison. Although some prison systems have adopted aggressive postures toward Muslim inmates, such heavy-handed policies run the risk of backfiring and fomenting radicalism, that is, "hysteric and stigmatizing reactions can fuel radicalization among prisoners and their followers, contributing to the threat rather than managing it." This is a lesson British prison officials have been learning since their extreme measures at security have inspired greater resistance among radicals.

Ultimately, administrators should explore how to harness the rehabilitative aspects of religion more than it has to the present. Religious education and fellowship opportunities should be developed and maintained by institutions without fearing establishment clause violations any more than a religious studies department at a state university would. The opportunity for religious study should be afforded to inmates as a programming scheme based on what helps released inmates stay out of prison. Such programming is different qualitatively from other educational opportunities due to the emphasis on morality and legal conduct. This is not just some area of study, but one that gets at the ultimate questions of life and meaning of existence. For followers of Islam in particular, formal religious education can have a direct impact in reducing radicalization, since, according to a recent report, "For radical Islamists, mainstream Islamic scholarship and ethics are a very real threat, perhaps the biggest threat." The opportunities for education in religious programming are valuable in themselves, but particularly because the educational outcomes converge with broader correctional goals and management of extremism.

Chapter 11

Religion as Rehabilitation?
Reflections on Islam in the Correctional Setting

I.   WHO IS A MUSLIM?

Although this question seems straightforward, defining Islam in the American context is sometimes difficult. Unlike in many parts of the world where Muslim populations have divisions that are clear-cut, in America the situation is more complex, with many groups identifying with Islam, including indigenous and immigrant varieties. In prison, the question is even more complicated, with more groups competing for and contesting the title of "Muslim," as well as by the emergence of so-called "prislam" groups which are defined by the interface of Islamic and gang culture.

As a baseline to addressing the question, one might be tempted to reduce Islam to a laundry list that includes reading the Quran, being born to Muslim parents, or praying five times a day facing east, yet many self-proclaimed Muslims fit none of the scripts. For example, since their inception, American groups like the Moorish Science Temple and the Nation of Islam (NOI) have long been viewed as non-Muslim, heretical, and blasphemous by Muslims from both the United States and abroad. The same holds true for the Five Percent Nation of Islam, which has been classified as a Security Threat Group by prison officials, rather than as a legitimate Islamic tradition. With such distinctions, it is clear that configuring the meaning of Islam is immensely important—and subjective. In the legal arena, courts have frequently reduced Islam to a set of "practices . . . largely unaffected by history or a change of context," which effectively puts the legal system out of sync with the realities of American Muslim beliefs and practices.

These realities signal a caution when treating "Muslim" or "Islam" through such a deterministic or essentialist frame. "Who" is Muslim may not be for the researcher to decide inasmuch as the believer who *self-identifies* as Islamic or Muslim. Following this line of reasoning, one scholar suggests that the student of Islam should not even insist on using a person's identification with the Qur'an as a kind of minimal definition of what it means to be a Muslim. Instead, wherever and whenever a person calls himself or herself Muslim, scholars should include this person's voice in their understanding of what constitutes Islam.

The idea of recognizing as Muslims all those who "self-identify as Muslims" is not a new concept, and is similar to identifying a "religious inmate" as one "who proclaims to practice and believe in one of the [recognized faiths]." This chapter heeds the warnings and adopts this more inclusive approach regarding who is a Muslim.

II. WHAT IS REHABILITATION?

Determining what is meant by the term "rehabilitation" is an equally difficult task, since its intents and purposes have changed with the times. Moreover, there are differences between advocates of rehabilitation about what the term means and whether it should be a goal of the criminal justice system. The root of the term (*re + habitare*) indicates making "fit" or "suitable," which in the penal setting generally describes the improvement of the individual, including restoring the inmate and restoring him back to society. Under the medical model in the mid-twentieth century, rehabilitation was premised on the view that the inmate was "sick" and required "treatment" to "cure" him of the malady. From this account, rehabilitation has expanded to include penal treatments aimed at "effect[ing] changes in the characters, attitudes, and behavior of convicted offenders." More broadly, however, taking up religion in prison may be likened to a type of education, and education is viewed by criminologists as generally conducive for successful rehabilitation and reentry. But taking up religion behind bars means more to inmates than just secular education, for Islam embodies a unique aspect of training and a quest to understand liturgy and doctrine; it can inspire one to take up reading for the first time or inspire one who struggled in junior high English, to teach himself Arabic.

At present, the hallmark of determining success in rehabilitation is the recidivism rate, or the rate at which formerly incarcerated individuals return to prison. Prison programming that focuses on preventing recidivism may thus be properly viewed as rehabilitative in approach, since it tries to improve an offender's prospects for remaining out of prison. However, using recidivism rates to determine successful inmate rehabilitation can lead to skewed results. For example, in some jurisdictions, recidivism rates represent violations of parole conditions rather than a new offense, which speaks less about rehabilitation than technicalities in "revolving door" or "catch and release" parole systems. In addition, mentally ill inmates are 80% likely to recidivate, which inflates these figures. Recidivism rates must thus be approached with caution since they can discount rehabilitation's success in fundamental ways.

There is little systematic research to assess the impact of religious programs in prison, a lack that is partially due to the nature of inquiry. Faith and redemption are difficult to measure, and ascertaining their contribution to rehabilitation is even more so. Noting the problem, one scholar explains that "faith in faith-based prison programs has been incorrectly tied to empirical findings from [a] social science, rather than to the true redemptive changes that occur in the lives of many participants in the programs." In addition to shortcomings in method, it is rarely the case that religion is the sole cause of conversion, but as mentioned, it is often one dimension of a multidimensional transformation, one of several important factors at play. For these reasons, religious conversion does not easily lend itself to empirical study.

This academic gap, however, should not obscure the fact that religion has proved a net good for prisoners and administrators alike, and has supported rehabilitation in fundamental ways. For example, one of the pioneering studies of American Islam noted that recovering alcoholic and drug-addicted inmates were able to cope more effectively after converting to Islam. More recent studies have determined that religious involvement can reduce prisoner misconduct and is a viable correctional intervention. The Department of Health and Human Services reports that literature on religion and recidivism "is consistent with criminological theories supporting the claim that religious beliefs are inversely related to delinquency, crime and recidivism." In the juvenile context, some researchers assert that high levels of participation in religious activities can reduce juvenile delinquency.

That Islam's relationship to rehabilitation is in want of further study is doubtless, yet a related inquiry is how Islam helps individuals rehabilitate from *the prison experience*. Note that this question is different from the ideas presented above since the focus is not on the individual's improvement but rather, in exorcising from the inmate the influences of prison culture, including the deprivations, psychological stress disorders, fear of violence, decreased mental health, and criminogenic influences. These issues are entirely different from those traditionally addressed by proponents of rehabilitation, but they must be considered if a fuller understanding of Islam's role in prison is to be attained. The fact remains, however, that some inmates use religion as a coping mechanism for prison itself, and not for their prior proclivities.

III. CONVERSION IN PRISON

"Conversion," as a general idea can imply a secular or religious transformation, which, in the religious context, indicates a belief transition in matters of "ultimate concern." It often involves a two-fold act of turning away from some aspects of life and adopting practices of the new religion. Some inmates embrace an ideology that is self-empowering and changes their negative outlook on life and behaviors, including praying and following a strict regime. In such instances, conversion represents a "process of identity change, potentially a total change of identity. It is a kind of rebirth . . . . for it involves a radical break with the past." Although conversion rarely results in a "total" change in one's personality, "it can result in profound, life transforming changes in mid-level functions such as goals, feelings, attitudes, and behaviors, and in the more self-defining personality functions such as identity and life meaning." Converts also employ religion as a tool for dissent and a framework for resistance, which can include adopting Islam as a foil to Christianity.

There are no reliable rates of conversion inside or outside of prison and no reliable statistics for the total number of Muslims in the United States or under incarceration. This state of affairs arises in part because the government does not track religion on Census surveys and because state prisons typically fail to track inmates' religious affiliation. Today's estimates suggest that there are 6 million Muslims in the United States. Other research contests these figures as inflated, including the Pew Research Center's estimate of 2.3 million, and most recently, University of Chicago researcher Tom Smith's review of prior national surveys that determined the adult Muslim population in 2000 was 1,886,000. One commentator estimates the American Muslim population to be 3 million, a figure arrived at by adopting the Pew figure and rounding up, while other scholars provide varying estimates of 4, 5.7, and 7 million, indicating nothing close to a consensus of census of the Muslim population.

Taken wholly, the available data on American Muslims and conversion offer some striking possibilities. For example, by dividing the upper estimate of 350,000 Muslim inmates by the lower estimate of 2.2 million Muslims in total, the figures suggest that over *fifteen percent of American Muslims are under incarceration*. This stunning figure makes the prison tower as a locus of conversion to Islam that contributes to Islam's overall growth. Such startling possibilities underscore the need for more research on this subject, including trying to achieve a more accurate count of prisoners.

IV. SUPPORTING INMATE REHABILITATION

Contrary to many of the warnings issued about Islam in prison, Muslim inmates influence prison culture in ways that support prospects for increasing rehabilitation and reducing recidivism. The most basic way that Muslims have done this is by institutionalizing Islam through litigation. Muslim inmates have become frontrunners in using courts to secure First Amendment rights to practice religion in prison and to contest conditions of confinement. These legal struggles have created space for inmates to practice Islam in prison, which facilitates preaching efforts from both inmates and religious leaders from the outside. Some inmates become attracted to Islam through the cultural connections in Africa and Spain, which can offer a new sense of self- identity, taking hopelessness and nihilism and replacing them with pride and self-esteem. Moreover, the discipline of Muslims has historically been a great attraction for inmates, who repeatedly mentioned that the regimented life instilled self-respect and faith in one's own ability. Still for others, the more practical elements of the religion are the draw, including worship and prayer practices, not to mention, Islam's influence in hip hop music, which is monumental for the spread of Islam.

BUILDING SELF-ESTEEM

For some inmates, Islamic history forges a pathway for African Americans to reconnect with their African roots and the Arabic language. These cultural aspects help to activate inmates by instilling a conception of their religious and cultural identity. Under such a worldview, some inmates find meaning in the fact that significant numbers of Muslims were among the Africans brought to America during the slave trade. This historical frame affords inmates a way to reflect on their identity and their incarceration as slavery in its own right, as an extension of the oppression endured by their religious ancestors. Equally compelling for African Americans is the narrative of the African ex-slave, Bilal, who was chosen by the Prophet Muhammad to call Muslims to pray for the first time. These connections allow inmates to get to the roots of identity, both as descendants of Africa and of Islam.

Islam also provides a gateway for individuals to connect to the rich tradition of conversion to Islam as it occurred in the American context. Islam's growth among African Americans traces back to the early 1900s, when groups like the Moorish Science Temple, the Nation of Islam, and followers of the Ahmadiyya movement began focusing their attention on outreach to African Americans. These denominations have produced some of the most prominent leaders in African- American history, including Elijah Muhammad, Malcolm X, and Louis Farrakhan. The story of an African-American man who goes to prison and converts to Islam is a cultural staple, the most influential of which is undisputedly Malcolm X. His story is cemented in African Americana and beyond: pop icons from Muhammad Ali to Michael Jackson represent some of the most famous converts, along with Mike Tyson, who himself converted in prison.

Like their African-American counterparts, Islam offers a sense of pride and self-esteem among Latino inmates, who adopt a similar cultural logic and embrace Islam as a way of reconnecting to their Spanish heritage. For Latinos, Islam is perhaps unlike any other religion due to historical factors similar to those that define the African-American experience. As the term "Moor" was embraced by various African-American leaders to unite the poor and disenfranchised with Islam, the Latino embrace of Moorish Spain provides a powerful tool to re-imagine identity. Followers learn about influences of Arabic on Spanish, that popular Latin American terms like *ojala* ("may God will") and *ole* come from the Arabic *allah*, and that surnames like "Medina" and "Mora" are proof of their Islamic ancestry. Islam connects Latinos to their Spanish heritage in ways beyond worship and doctrine; when Latinos convert it is more than the adoption of a new religion, but sometimes, something more profound—a reconnecting to an ancient cultural pedigree.

The intersections of Islam and Spanish and African history afford inmates a powerful way of positively re-imagining their identity as inherently Islamic. Exactly how this cultural revival influences the prison environment is still unknown, but for many inmates, the identification with Islam and Moorish Spain and Africa has positive impacts on self-esteem and self-respect, which undoubtedly complement the goals of rehabilitation as necessary conditions for success. With insufficient self-esteem, rehabilitation is impossible, but with faith in oneself, one can at least strive to make a change.

SPEAKING THROUGH HIP HOP CULTURE

For many, hip hop/rap culture facilitates the turn to Islam. Since the birth of hip hop, Muslim producers and rap artists have been a part of the culture, mixing in Islamic names, themes, and symbols. Muslims collectively comprise the most important voices in hip hop culture, and have given us expressions like "word" and "what up, G?" as well as the pervasive term, "peace," influencing both the hip hop lexicon and that of mainstream America. Hip hop music is a major conduit for the spread of Islam in America, and according to one scholar, "The hip- hop movement's role in popularizing the message of black militant Islam cannot be overestimated. What reggae was to the expansion of the Rastafarian movement in the 1970s, so hip-hop is to the spread of black Islam in the 1980s and 1990s." For many youth, hip hop music "leads to their first encounter with Islam, and often leads them to struggle with issues of race, identity, and Western imperialism." Although some listeners may not be aware of or interested in the religious underpinnings of the music, the references have brought Islamic themes and symbols to the American ghettos, barrios, and suburbs beyond. One scholar asserts that the music has "special appeal" for prisoners in particular, which may reflect many rappers' focus on the prison, a trend that may be due to the NOI's significant impact on hip culture.

TRANSITIONING INDIVIDUALS FROM GANG CULTURE

Islam also supports rehabilitation by offering gang-members an alternative to the gang lifestyle. A significant number of individuals come to Islam from gang life, yet little is known about the relationship between Islam and gang culture. One scholar notes that "[r]arely if at all, mentioned in social science studies is the influence of religious conversion in a youth's ability to leave the gang." This gap in part may be due to the difficult task of measuring religious conversion; nonetheless, many of those who are now law-abiding Muslims were once gangsters, a transformation elsewhere described as "Gangland Gangstas Turning Gods." How Islam helps individuals transition from the gang life awaits further study, but one researcher suggests that in some ways, "religion functions similar to gang affiliation and the need to connect to other people." One might also speculate that the idea of Islam as a "warrior religion" may also resonate with gang members. Regardless of our lack of knowledge, there is little doubt that the religion has found an audience among gangsters, as depicted famously by the Crips leader Monster Kody Scott, who reflected on his own transformation in prison: "I was changing, I felt it. For once I didn't challenge it or see it as being a threat to the established mores of the 'hood, though, of course, it was. Muhammad's teachings corresponded with my condition of being repressed on the Rock. Never could I have been touched by such teachings in the street."

INSTILLING DISCIPLINE

Islam supports rehabilitation by instilling inmates with a greater sense of discipline. This contribution is important for the criminal justice system since it results in a more orderly prison environment and facilitates prison administration. This aspect of religious practice was noted in a pioneering study on prisons in the Northeast, which indicated that the NOI helped inmates with morale, discipline, and rehabilitation. Other studies have found that religious converts fared better with prison adjustment, reduced stress, increased self-esteem, and better reformatory potential. Some scholarship asserts that Islam has transformed many convicts into upstanding citizens, citing the Muslim prisoners who protected guards during the Attica and Sing Sing riots or figures that suggest Muslims enjoy a lower recidivism rate than other religious groups nationwide.

African Americans authors note the sustained discipline of Muslims in their preaching efforts. For example, Malcolm X's time in prison in the 1950s was characterized by outreach efforts of the NOI. In his 1965 autobiography, Claude Brown raises the question rather seriously: "Damn . . . what the hell is going on in the jails here? It seems that everybody who comes out is a Muslim." In the 1970s, Eldridge Cleaver noted Muslims' dedication to spreading Islam: "Every black inmate was exposed to the Black Muslim teachings . . . it was not a rare sight to see several Muslims walking around the yard, each with a potential convert." Three decades later, Nathan McCall's autobiography notes how preaching efforts are as focused as ever: "No African American spends much time in prison without being exposed to the doctrines of black Muslims . . . Brothers respected [the] Muslims for being disciplined, religious people and, at the same time, warriors."

V. CONCLUSIONS

Religion tends to correlate with positive penal outcomes among inmates, and Islam in particular is noteworthy in this respect. As such, prison administrators might offer more support for religious programming and consider its utility as a correctional strategy. Instead of simply being a constitutional right to be afforded inmates, religion might be seen as a type of evidence-based programming that forwards the goal of inmate rehabilitation. In many instances, Islam appears more successful at rehabilitating inmates than other state-sanctioned programs, and so officials should work to harness some of this power.

Although it is difficult to measure religion's influence on an inmate's positive adjustment or successful transition to society, lack of empirical data should not deter prison officials from supporting religion in prison and outside. Despite the lack of hard data, one researcher stresses the enormous potential that faith based services have to offer the correctional systems and cultures in the United States. Similarly, the Department of Health and Human Services suggests that "religious programming may be uniquely suited to both facilitate and augment the ongoing process of prison reentry." For jurisdictions that approach corrections as a collaborative effort involving the community, this might encourage programs to parole Muslims into stable religious communities. Although this is easier said than done, there are already many mosques throughout the United States doing this type of work on their own, but more could be achieved with support from the state.

Chapter 12

Sonic Jihad:
Muslim Hip Hop in the Age of Mass Incarceration

Sidelines of chairs neatly divide the center field and a large stage stands erect. At its center, there is a stately podium flanked by disciplined men wearing the militaristic suits of the Fruit of Islam, a visible security squad. This is Ford Field, usually known for housing the Detroit Lions football team, but on this occasion it plays host to a different gathering and sentiment.

The seats are mostly full, both on the floor and in the stands, but if you look closely, you'll find that this audience isn't the standard sporting fare: the men are in smart suits, the women dress equally so, in long white dresses, gloves, and headscarves. These are the members of the new Nation of Islam, and they are waiting for their leader to take stage. After a brief introductory speech, the speaker, Ishmael Muhammad, announces: "Here is the Honorable Minister Louis Farrakhan!"

"Allahu Akbar" translates to "God is great." It is a call that has become widely recognized and associated with extremist Muslims in recent years, but chances are you haven't heard it quite like this. The gathered crowd chants in rapid succession. "Allahu Akbar!" "Long live Muhammad!" "Farrakhan, Farrakhan!" The crowd then erupts into applause as Farrakhan stands before the pulpit. This is Saviours' Day, the biggest event of the year for the Nation of Islam (NOI). The year 2007 is the 77th anniversary of the NOI, and Farrakhan is visibly pleased to see so many believers before him. He addresses them softly, like a kindly grandfather, as his "brothers and sisters."

Everyone before him is a brother or a sister under the wide umbrella of Islam, and today is a day for building bridges. Upon the stage with him is a flock of "distinguished guests . . . teachers, scholars, theologians, pastors, Imams, politicians, businessmen, and artists." To his left, sit these distinguished guests from the outside world, and to his right, sit a group of equally distinguished members of the NOI itself. His speech is heartfelt, his smile broad.

Farrakhan's words at Saviours Day 2007 are a lesson in how to reach the youth—and focusing on what works. As radio and television have offered black children a poor set of role models, Farrakhan has sharp words for showbiz; yet at the same time, he is conscious of what famous people can do for the NOI—after all, when Malcolm X helped convert the boxer Cassius Clay into "Muhammad Ali," it was a powerful push for the organization. Thus instead of simply shunning entertainment, Farrakhan chooses a different route, one that finds a place for rap music in God's work:

> Hip-hop is an art, and don't you talk down on it just because it has something in it that may not be to our liking. Talk up to it, because the hip-hop artist is the new leader. He leads the people wrong, but the same leader that leads them wrong can lead them right if you put the right message in their heads and in their hearts. Let's go get our hip-hop artists! Let's break the bond between these destructive CEO's and producers that tell conscious lyricists that that's not going to sell and force them to do filthy lyrics in the name of selling filth to our people.

Farrakhan's aim is not to shun art, but rather to embrace it. His plan is not simply to accept hip hop as an artistic form and means of spreading the faith, but beyond, to try to convert those hip hoppers who are already famous. Farrakhan's approach is an active mission: "Let's go get our hip- hop artists!" This attitude likely helps to account for Islam's continued success in hip hop culture and the respect Farrakhan holds.

By the end of his speech, Farrakhan effectively portrays hip hop culture as an important part of recruitment efforts. His attitude makes the rap world not just fair game for preaching efforts, but a main target, just as prisons are. For a genre of music that is shunned by many in a manner similar to the way prisoners are shunned by society, Farrakhan sees something else. For those familiar with hip hop and prison history, what he sees is clear: Islamic symbols, names, and ideology have infused the very core of hip hop and prison culture. The history traces to Farrakhan's teacher, Elijah Muhammad, whose message spread rapidly in American penitentiaries beginning in the 1950s. The fusion of these creative forces would create a cadre of holy warriors with an artistic message bent on chanting down walls that hold many of their brethren captive.

I.   THE HIP HOP GENERATION: DOWN BY LAW

When interpreting hip hop lyrics, a few heuristics are worth noting. As a general matter, hip hop might be best understood as a strategy of resistance. In addition to resisting racial or religious discrimination, gangs, or poverty, the music has been instrumental in conveying black oppression and discontent with the law:

> Hip-hop exposes the current punishment regime as profoundly unfair. It demonstrates this view by, if not glorifying law breakers, at least not viewing all criminals with the disgust which the law seeks to attach to them. Hip-hop points out the incoherence of the law's construct of crime, and it attacks the legitimacy of the system.

Another key insight is the temporal relationship between hip hop culture and the growth of prisons. When hip hop culture first took root in the late 1970s, the country had just embarked on what would become a decades-long punishment spree, with billions in state funds going to correctional budgets. Hip hop was a late twin to this new penal boom. Like its counterpart, the music became a huge financial moneymaker, generating billions for record companies and publishing houses. The two were somewhat symbiotic since effects of mass imprisonment were felt directly by the hip hop generation and its offspring, who were subject to the law like no other demographic. "Whether blacks or Latinos, young men or women, hip hop's youth found themselves—or someone close—chained to a correctional system and culture determined to mete out severe punishment."

Cursing and Killing Cops

In hip hop slang, the "law" often refers to police, which is a collective source of animosity in hip hop culture. The relationship between hip hop and law enforcement is profound, and according to one interpretation of KRS-One's "Sound of da Police," "policing Black people is actually the cornerstone of anti-Blackness under American law." Pharoahe Monch drives the point home rhetorically: "What is the law? Know you heard this before. We find contraband in your car, we break in your jaw."

Authored by some of the most influential acts in hip hop history, the songs center on the evils of cops brutalizing youth in poor, ethnic minority neighborhoods. Perhaps the greatest hip hop anthem of anti-police songs is NWA's "Fuck that Police," a satire of courtroom proceedings conducted by street rules. In this sketch, the group puts the police on trial in the case of "NWA v. the Police Department," with Dr. Dre presiding as judge and Ice Cube taking oath and offering the first testimony: "Fuck the police, coming straight from the underground. A young nigga got it bad cause I'm brown. And not the other color so police think they have the authority to kill a minority." This unblinking stance toward police brutality paved the way for other indictments, including when rapper Ice T and his band, Bodycount, released the song "Cop Killer." It instantaneously sparked widespread political discontent that eventually forced their record label to remove the song from the album. The song's hook pulls no punches: "I'm a cop killer, better you than me. Cop killer, fuck police brutality. Cop killer, I know your family's grieving, fuck em! Cop killer, but tonight we get even." Megastar rapper Tupac Shakur likewise shared no love for police and was an outspoken critic as "Fuck the Police" declares: "Punk police can't fade me—you made me, crooked ass-beast something daisy. But right now I got my mind set up, looking down the barrel of my nine. Get up! Cause it's time to make that pay back. Fact." In equally descriptive fashion, 50 Cent vows:

> Police get in the way, I'll murder them, I'll Murder them
> A nigga already got three strikes, I'll murder them, I said I'll murder them
> Any motherfucker touch me, I'll murder them, I'll murder them You don't believe me wait and see, I'll murder them
> You see, I told you I'd murder them.

Punishing Prisons

Like lyrics condemning crooked cops, in hip hop lyrics one does not have to dig much to find some story about the penitentiary. There are countless songs that condemn prisons and the hardships they breed, as well as whole albums dedicated to their demise, and even groups like Down by Law and State Property, whose identities reflect the importance of the penal system in hip hop consciousness. In Why are So Many Black Men in Prison?, one ex-prisoner offers his view on the breadth of prison's influence:

> The subliminal messages sent by an extremely large portion of today's premier urban movies, rap and R&B songs, and music videos, if you are conscious and observative enough to notice, shows just how predominant prison is in our reality. Almost every Black song or video references prison or jail in one way or another.

Although this might overstate the case, the prominence of prisons in the music goes all the way back to the phrase "down by law." The phrase has been a staple in hip hop since Grandmaster Flash and the Furious Five's pioneering album, The Message in 1982. The Message is particularly important in this regard since the album put prisons front and center as one of the greatest problems facing black youth. The album's namesake song delivers a scathing critique of life in the ghetto and made the brutal realities of prison all too real for the hip hop generation. One passage describes a youth who is convicted for robbery and sentenced to eight years of prison. His experience quickly deteriorates after being forced into sex slavery, "being used and abused and served like hell, till one day [he] was found hung dead in a cell." Described as "one of the most important songs in hip hop history," the message made clear to the hip hop generation that prisons were a menacing threat.

Later artists followed in their predecessors' footsteps and took criticism of prisons to new heights. Rappers like Dead Prez have written multiple songs detailing the ills of imprisonment, including "Police State," which situates imprisonment within a greater racial struggle: "The average black male live[s] a third of his life in a jail cell cause the world is controlled by the white male." Ludacris' "Do your Time" tells of stark realities behind bars: "It's slavery, hard labor, catch the feel. Redneck on the hearse while you walk, it's real. With a shotgun, burnin' at the back of your dome 300 years left, my dawg ain't never comin' home." Hussein Fatal's "Prison" tells of the harsh environment where even hardened individuals break down: "In prison is similar to dying, where a gangster can get a pass if he in his cell crying." Such lyrics attest to the special space prisons occupy in hip hop consciousness and provide a backdrop for the next section, which focuses on Muslim artists.

II. THE GODS OF HIP HOP

In the world of hip hop, Islamic influences cannot be overstated. Muslim rappers from different denominations bring prophetic and charismatic voices to the culture in the name of promoting peace, love, and self-realization, while extreme varieties tend toward apocalyptic brands of faith, steeped in gangster isms and the rhetoric of retribution. Muslim artists represent some of the most influential, best-selling, and widely known entertainers in hip hop music, who have helped steer the course of hip hop history.

Islamic Attitudes Towards Prisoners

Before delving straight into the lyrics, it is worth considering traditional Islamic attitudes toward prisoners. This approach provides a useful lens for interpreting the music and lyrics. The religious underpinnings of the faith reveal multiple rationales at stake for Muslims to oppose prisons. Thus, beyond the mere fact that many Muslims are incarcerated, resisting prisons may have more divine implications.

Passages in the Quran intimately link the treatment of prisoners to spiritual consciousness. Verses signal out kindness to captives as a virtue and means of eradicating sins, and as a means of exercising piety. The message of Sura 90:10–13 offers a telling lesson in this regard: "Did we not show him the two paths? He should choose the difficult path. Which one is the difficult path? The freeing of slaves."

The scripture equates the freeing of slaves with the "difficult" path—which obviously can be interpreted literally or figuratively. There is also verse 9:60 that prescribes how *zakah* or alms should be spent: "Zakah expenditures are only for the poor and for the needy and for those employed to collect [zakah] and for bringing hearts together and for freeing captives . . . ." One commentator has interpreted this passage to indicate hierarchy in the ransoming of prisoners over slaves: "Ransoming Muslim prisoners who have been captured by kaafirs is better than freeing slaves, so it is included [in the zakah] and indeed takes priority, because they suffer great harm by being separated from their families and because of the humiliation and torture. So saving them is even more important than saving slaves."

There are other cultural connections. For example, one scholar notes that "Malik, the founder of the Maliki School, allows Muslims to visit the lands of the infidels for one purpose only—to ransom captives." This religious duty was not lost in hip hop when Mujahideen Team referred to itself as "technicians of a Maliki tradition" in the song "Dead Has Risen." As a song focused on ransoming "soldiers locked down making juma in prison," the group has built on this idea to create a clear sense of its identity as "slave-emancipators."

Contemporary views among Muslims reflect similar values. For example, the NOI has been at the fore of prison outreach and has been setting prisoners "free" in the spiritual sense for decades. Such Muslim outreach undoubtedly contributes to the widespread conversion to Islam among African-American prisoners. In addition, the organization has been outspoken in its opposition to mass incarceration. On its list of "What the Muslims want," the NOI for years has listed: "We want freedom for all Believers of Islam now held in federal prisons. We want freedom for all black men and women now under death sentence in innumerable prisons in the North as well as the South. Such a position seems tame compared to a more recent statement in 2013 by Al-Qaeda leader, Ayman al-Zawahri, who vowed to set prisoners free from the American-run Guantanamo Bay prison: "We pledge God that we will spare no efforts to set them free along with all our prisoners . . . and every oppressed Muslim everywhere."

Two Decades of Blasting

These early attitudes resonated with later generations of artists. Perhaps the most forceful statement against the prison system would come just a few years later in 1988 with Public Enemy's album, *It Takes a Nation of Millions to Hold Us Back*. The album features a bold graphic of the group behind prison bars and classics like "Black Steel in the Hour of Chaos." Perhaps the crown jewel of anti-prison raps, this song tells about a prison escape inspired by unbearable prison conditions:

> They got me rotting in the time that I'm serving
> Telling you what happened the same time they're throwing Four of us packed in a cell like slaves—oh well
> The same motherfucker got us living in his hell You have to realize that it's a form of slavery Organized under a swarm of devils

A decade later, Nas would tell of haunting despair in "Last Words," which creatively flips the artistic angle by telling the story from the *prison's* perspective: "I'm a prison cell six by nine. Living hell stone wall metal bars for the gods in jail. My nickname the can, the slammer, the big house. I'm the place many fear cause there's no way out." This solitary chamber, however, has more to say about the too many inmates who fall apart inside its confines:

> When you cry I make you feel alive inside a coffin
> Watch you when you eat play with your mind when
> you sleep Make you dream that you free, then make
> you wake up to me Face to face with a cage, no matter
> your age
> I can shatter you, turn you into a savage in a rage

The year after this song's release, rapper Beanie Sigel contributed a similarly chilling classic focused on the maddening dullness of day-to-day existence. Likely reflecting some of his own experiences while incarcerated, his technique in "What Ya Life Like?" asks the listener a string of questions that juxtaposes prison life with normal existence:

> What you know about solitary? Locked down, no
> commissary . . . What you know about no parole? Life
> in the hole Life's cold, you be eatin' them swags
> Guards on the nightshift beatin' you bad
> The hardest nigga turned bitch, sleepin' with fags

In the sequel to this song, Sigel continues the theme, but rather than quizzing the ignorant, the rhetorical approach is reversed and the questions are posed to one who knows:

> Can you tell me what you live like?
> Can you tell me what that bed like, what's that cell
> like?
> What's livin in hell like? Tell me do you eat right?
> Do you even sleep right?
> Yo, tell me what your life like
> Tell me do you sleep nights, tell me what that life like?
> Gettin no kites like, no flicks like
> Make you wanna quit life

Expressions After Terror

The above lyrics capped a golden era of prison raps, yet the culture would take a turn after the 2001 attacks in New York City. Attitudes toward imprisonment both by Muslims and Muslim sympathizers took on a decidedly more menacing countenance. This qualitative difference may be traced to the social and political backlash against Muslims in America that followed the attacks. Artists like Immortal Technique, Paris, Mujahideen Team, and other rappers in this vein unleashed a verbal rampage that has been dubbed "jihadi" rap for its firebrand lyrics. The lyrics talk of suicide bombings, attacking the White House, and setting prisoners free, all of which signals a break from longstanding hip hop critiques, since previously the discourse focused on telling the pains of prison—now the radicalism was infused with greater political urgency.

As a result of political events, hip hop's radical posture toward prisons was further radicalized. On the fringes of hip hop lyricism bubbled a cadre of rappers who pushed the boundaries of free speech. Among these individuals, Immortal Technique emerged as one of the most militant. Although it is uncertain if he himself holds sectarian views, Technique has been an avid commentator on Muslim issues, and was himself previously incarcerated as he indicates:

> This is the point of no return I could never go back Life without parole, up state shackled and trapped Living in the hole looking at the world through a crack. A suicide bomber strapped down ready to blow, Lethal injection strapped down ready to go.

Even ultra-radicals like Jedi Mind Tricks took time from their lyrics of punishment and vengeance to showcase the prison's moneymaking aspects in "Shadow Business":

> It's 1.6 million people locked in jail
> They the new slave labor force, trapped in hell They generate over a billion dollars' worth of power And only gettin' paid twenty cents an hour
> They make clothes for McDonald's and for Applebee's And workin' forty-hour shifts in prison factories . . .
> Slavery's not illegal, that's a fuckin' lie

It's illegal, unless it's for conviction of a crime

Although the figure quoted by now is well over two million, "Trigger" helps to explain the driving force behind such numbers:

> Homeland security, political impurity
> Governmental crackdown quick to put the smackdown
> Hide away the gat now before they come rush us The
> 21st century got too many pressures Anxious and
> scared and their plans to depress us
> Nowhere to confess because they watch us with
> sensors Life is the sentence when you fail to obey
> Better take a holiday, run away like OJ

Mujahideen Team also raps about a day when friends and "soldiers" come home from prison and live a life in Islam:

> Coming home out of the jails, out of the prisons, out of
> the slave plantations man
> Welcome home, all my soldiers that were locked
> Welcome home free from the prison blocks Welcome
> home, a fresh new start from the past Keep your head
> up and stay on the straight path Welcome home, all my
> soldiers that were locked Welcome home free from the
> prison blocks
> Welcome home, a fresh new start from the past Keep
> your head up and stay on the straight path

Lupe Fiasco has been equally outspoken about the harms of prison and equally torn from the impacts. In "Free Chilly," a tearful serenade to those on lockdown, he focuses on forgiveness and the prospects of reunion with lost comrades: "If we could break down those walls to set you free, we would cause we're out here, and we miss you." More recently, Fiasco's "Prisoners 1 & 2" offers a creative pièce de résistance, which begins with the prerecorded message of a collect call from prisoner number one:

> Getting slammed from the protest, no food Force fed
> him like OB with a nose tube
> I'm just looking at they feet, cause I'm looking for the
> lord Looking in the library, looking at the law
> 10 years deep now I'm looking at the bars

Claim sovereignty because I'm bunkin' with the moors

In this prisoner's plight, the law offers little succor. Still, he manages to find relief by associating with the "moors," which is shorthand for Muslims. Prisoner number two offers a striking contrast since it is not about a prisoner serving a sentence, but a racist guard who is likened to an inmate: "You a prisoner too, you living here too. You just like us, til your shift get through. You could look like us, you know shit get through. You should be in cuffs like us, you should get strike two." Among the accusations is the prospect that the correctional officer is a smuggler and should be behind bars with the inmate as a resident rather than as staff. The point is obvious—despite their positions—the prisoner may be freer than the guard, who in turn may be more criminal.

Although recording artists resist imprisonment primarily through their music, an original protest came from Yasiin Bey (also known as Mos Def) in 2013. Bey voluntarily agreed to undergo the force-feeding process to which prisoners are subjected at the American prison at Guantanamo Bay. The recording of this event had to be stopped at Bey's request, who could no longer endure the procedure. A sobbing Bey is shown at the end in a daze, at which point one is not sure if it is from what he just experienced or the thought of those who must go through it for real.

III. CONCLUSION: LESSONS IN WAR & PEACEMAKING

Some of the most extreme discourse in America appears in hip hop's criticism of the law. Muslim artists have been dropping bombs on police and prisons for decades, and have particularly pushed the heights of imagery and creativity in the name of slaying the beast.

Although Muslim fundamentalists are notorious for speeches built on fierce religious rhetoric, American hip hoppers are equally adept at battling with words. For example, invocations of Muslim sisters and daughters being violated are a longtime tool of extremist rhetoric. Yet hip hoppers have mastered the technique, as in "Day of Retribution," a call to war that imitates what one might hear at a protest march in the Middle East. This procession, however, is taking place on American soil, and the man blaring on the megaphone is not speaking in Arabic, but English:

> Oh you sons and daughters of Adam! Oh you brave and righteous souls! Today is the day of retribution. Today

is the day that the devil has raised his head; he has undressed his sword; he has decorated his blade with the sacred blood of your brothers; he has violently violated the sanctity of your sisters. Today is the day of retribution. Today is the day of jihad. Today is the day of victory or martyrdom. So oh you who believe, raise your head and ready your weapon!

As such cultural productions illustrate, hip hop lyrics represent some of the most extremist speech at play in American society. In this arena, Muslim artists have emerged as leaders against a foe that continues to swallow individuals and communities whole. In this struggle, rappers need no assistance from their religious brethren abroad; they bring a history of rapping over beats rooted in slave spirituals that stretches all the way to Africa.

Part IV

Advancing Law, Policy, and Scholarship

The final set of chapters looks to the future by considering ways to right some of the problems highlighted throughout this anthology. Having offered a critical account of prison culture in America, including the challenges for law and society, this part concentrates on reform in these areas and reform in scholarship.

Included in this section are a number of critiques and prescriptive elements to assuage the crisis issues exposed throughout the book. It begins with a critique of the Supreme Court's "evolving standards of decency" doctrine, which is likened to a species of Social Darwinism. Despite the appeal of this benevolent-sounding moniker, this doctrine has little to say about how long an individual can be imprisoned or how long solitarily confinement may be imposed, which make it nearly useless for prisoners. The next chapter focuses on the question of prison's negative impacts on Latino communities. It shows that prison culture is intimately tied to the communities to which prisoners return, and that prisons are formidable foes for these communities. Next, the focus turns to the question of Muslim radicalization in prison, which has been a recurring drumbeat from Islamophobes in America since the attacks of 9/11. However, this chapter argues that these fears are based on alarmist rationales and faulty logic. Indeed, the available research suggests that prisons are not breeding grounds for an American Al-Qaeda movement or other such terror recruitment. Finally, is a scholarly critique of Mark Hamm's "The Spectacular Few: Prisoner Radicalization and the Evolving Terrorist Threat." As this is the first book of its kind dedicated exclusively to prisoner radicalization, it is critiqued as lagging in theoretical and methodological rigor, which produces faulty data, distorted truths, and clouding of the issues. Moving forward, as for political leaders, it will be critical to hold research and scholarship accountable for such shortcomings, lest entire religions become vilified in the attempt to understand these issues.

Chapter 13

Evolving Standards of Domination:
A Case for Killing Doctrine and Reinterpreting
"Cruel and Unusual"

INTRODUCTION

This chapter contends that "evolving standards of decency" provided a system of review that was tailor-made for Civil Rights opponents to scale back racial progress. Although as a doctrinal matter, evolving standards sought to tie punishment to social mores, prison sentencing fell prey to political agendas that determined the course of punishment more than the benevolence of a maturing society. The Court's evolutionary model was betrayed by decisions that allowed states nearly unfettered authority over prison sentencing and use of solitary confinement, a self-fulfilling prophecy of sorts. The expanded incarceration of poor, uneducated, minorities—the very population that might be expected under an evolutionary frame—was a deep irony. The Court ought to abandon evolving standards as a flawed and pernicious concept, and simultaneously, accept the duty to reinterpret the Eighth Amendment for prison sentencing and solitary confinement. The Court must move beyond its obsessive tinkering with the death penalty and focus on the realities of "doing time" in America.

I.   CRITICAL INSIGHTS INTO PUNISHMENT LAW IN THE PRESENT

Social Darwinism in the Judiciary

This section identifies the theoretical underpinnings of what is being termed "social Darwinism" as a means of understanding how evolving standards of decency fits within the concept. It also offers a substantive critique of the doctrine and the social implications of the doctrine's adoption, and particularly, normalization of the view that poor, uneducated, and other marginalized portions of society are indeed the people who belong in prison.

The label "social Darwinism," which derives from Charles Darwin's influence on social science, describes a movement that greatly influenced American jurisprudence: "For many of the new social scientists Darwin's natural selection model invited economic determinism—the idea that resource scarcity explains everything that happens." Particularly, it was Herbert Spencer, a contemporary evolutionary theorist, who coined the term "survival of the fittest," which was grounded in the notion that competition induced human beings to adapt themselves to their environments, improving mental and physical skills, which was then inherited by their descendants. This perspective veered somewhat from Darwin's model since "in the struggle for existence, self-improvement came from conscious, planned exertion, not from the chance variation and natural selection that are the heart of Darwinism. As a result, evolution is progressive in Spencer, whereas, for Darwin, at least the early Darwin, evolution means only non-teleological change." For Spencer, "[h]uman perfection [was] not only possible but inevitable." Social Darwinists thus clung to the assumption "that evolution by natural selection was a theory of 'progress' and should therefore be valued for its own sake."

The foundational aspects may be distilled to two major ingredients. The first is that people have intrinsic abilities that will manifest independent of social, economic, and cultural environments. Second, intense competition enables the most talented to develop their potential to make life better for all. Inherent in this worldview is a human culture that progresses through fierce competition, given that leaders do not support backward policy that protects the weak Accordingly, "[t]he most popular catchwords of Darwinism, 'struggle for existence' and 'survival of the fittest,' when applied to the life of man in society, suggested that nature would provide that the best competitors in a competitive situation would win, and that this process would lead to continuing improvement."

Survival of the Fittest?

As history demonstrates, dramatic increases in incarceration that began in the 1970s were part of conscious political campaigns to scale back victories of the Civil Rights Movement. Instead of the fierce competition espoused by social Darwinists, the political manipulation of the justice system produced *false* competition. Criminal defendants and their communities instead were made to face additional obstacles in competing with the rest of society that had little to do with natural phenomena and everything to do with oppression. The developments suggest that the "fittest" are so just because they wield the awesome power of the criminal justice system; far from developing along natural selection lines, punishment was a tool for some to keep others down—on lockdown, to be specific.

II. ABANDONING SOCIAL MYTH

Social Darwinists believed that genetics determined criminal behavior, and that nothing reformed the 'criminal type'; instead the criminal should be placed where he could not harm society.

--Herbert Hovenkamp from
Evolutionary Models in Jurisprudence

The evolving standards doctrine distorts punishment law and must be abandoned. As a legal standard, it is as unprincipled as unpredictable, and hardly helps advocates or lower courts do their work. Moreover, with the United States wielding "the most punitive criminal justice system in the modern industrialized world," the time has never been riper to make moves to retire as the world leader in incarceration. This current state of mass imprisonment resonates little with the notion of evolving standards of decency, and instead cripples economically weak communities that already struggle with high rates of intergenerational crime and poverty. As the doctrine leads to the sort of pain and misery the constitutional framers sought to limit, there are compelling reasons to reject it, and move forward with the task of interpreting the Constitution. The foundational deficiencies make it unworkable as a guide for determining proportionality, and by extension, cruel and unusual punishment.

III. TOWARD NEXT-ERA PENOLOGY

As this chapter contends, under evolving standards, the Court abdicated its task of determining "cruel and unusual" for prison sentencing and solitary confinement. The aftermath of this hands-off approach led to a decades-long punishment binge that has become the ultimate set-back for civil rights progress, which paradoxically occurred in the name of progress: "The actions and omissions of legislative bodies and executive agencies have created the impetus for judicial intervention." The case for intervention is bolstered by the fact that the Constitution does not detail the proper relationship between the three branches of government with much specificity, nor does it outline the relationship between the federal government and states. Hence, "there is no compelling reason why concerns about propriety and capacity should dominate the judicial function, especially if constitutional rights are being violated. It is a mistake to view each governmental branch as a separate actor with easily defined, narrowly focused functions." The point is important for this work since the U.S. Sentencing Commission lies at the center of implementing a science-based approach to sentencing duration.

The Imperative to Interpret "Unusual"

The first step entails the Court taking on the task of interpreting "unusual" as requiring something distinct from "cruel." In the past, members of the Court have expressed doubt as to whether the word has any qualitative meaning different from "cruel," dismissed the import of the word as of minor significance, described the word as "inadvertent," and most drastically, stated that it cannot be read as limiting the ban on "cruel" punishments. This failure has been critiqued for defying basic statutory construction that makes the conjunctive "and" the basis for an additional elementary requirement. It represents an additional restraint on government power and must not be ceded by omission. In the exceptional instances when the Court has bothered interpreting the term, it has typically understood it as an objective measure of the novelty or foreignness of a punishment. From this perspective, "unusual" punishments were measured against practices of the common law.

Using Research to Reinterpret "Cruel" and Recalibrate the Scales

An affirmative finding that imprisonment is an unusual punishment renders critical the question of when a sentence crosses the threshold of "cruel." This chapter asserts that rather than continue to tether punishment to the vagaries of the evolving standards doctrine, the Court must now do what has never been done before in American penal history—obligate federal and state governments to justify the scale of prison sentencing with scientific study. Such a stance would inaugurate a revolution in penology. As legislatures have been free of the obligation to justify sentence lengths, they have gone on to author some of the longest prison sentences in the world. It is thus long over-due to reconsider how long is too long. Even though there is a dearth of empirical research on this point, there is a need to know when imprisonment results in diminishing returns for the human psyche and ultimately for society. Although it has been decades since the Stanford Prison Experiment gave a glimpse of how quickly conditions can deteriorate for "inmates" when punishment power goes unchecked, the Court has never inquired into the empirical basis for assigning a given amount of time to a crime.

To assert that punishment law in the United States has never been guided by the findings of rigorous research and study may seem radical, but it is hardly so. The primary reference point for punishment has been the common law, including punishments like the stocks, whippings, pillories, branding, banishing, and other corporal punishments. However, with the turn to incarceration beginning in the early 1800s, incarceration has become the dominant mode of corporal punishment, which entailed a shift in calculus to determine punishment, since the focus was previously on how much pain was appropriate, whereas in imprisonment, the question was how much time was appropriate. In determining how long sentences should be, lawmaking has been steeped in arbitrariness with nothing close to a justification for assigning a certain amount of time for a particular crime. Still, it has been several decades since one researcher noted, "[I]t is uncontested that no prisoner can endure more than 15 years without fundamental damage to his personality."

Despite such admonitions, use of scientific studies plays a limited role in determining whether a punishment is "cruel" for Eight Amendment purposes. Even though the Court seeks objectivity, at times, scientific knowledge has been shunned directly by the Court, as in *Rhodes v. Chapman*, which overturned a District Court's ruling that Arkansas prisons were violating the Eighth Amendment. In that case, the lower court rooted its assessment of contemporary standards in several published works by practitioners in the field that recommended more space than the double bunking permitted. Here, the Court demonstrated the instability of evolving standards since the Court flatly rejected the objective recommendations of experts in the field. Thus, even though in *Trop*, the opinion propounded that punishment should be judged "in light of the contemporary human knowledge," this promise has gone largely unfulfilled.

This chapter explains how the judicial morass of evolving standards leads to real human suffering. The Court's embrace of evolutionary principles in its cruel and unusual jurisprudence allows full abdication of the duty to render a just interpretation of the Eighth Amendment for prison sentencing purposes, and facilitates the greatest rise in imprisonment the United States has ever known. The power to incarcerate became a matter of legislative fiat with only the sky as the limit. In these decades, the Court has engaged in pseudo-science on multiple levels, including the embrace of progressive evolutionary theory, its application to society, and its means of ascertaining the content of social norm. It is past time for the Court to relinquish these machinations and look to scientific study and research for the objectivity it has been seeking all along.

Exactly what model of social organization should supplant the current adherence to social Darwinism is uncertain, but whatever that understanding is, it must have a more skeptical countenance than the rosy-red teleology of evolving standards. It should be particularly vigilant in matters related to legal punishment since the power to punish has been described as "protean force that is eminently fertile and must be given pride of place in the study of contemporary power." From this principle, it is clear that the criminal justice system is always at risk of appropriation to the ends of power rather than justice. Moreover, making the determination is fraught with subjectivity, which can be legitimated only when "rule is governed by articulable and reproducible objective standards." This reality makes judicial review of punishment an absolute, ongoing necessity. Yet, for far too long the Court has been preoccupied with death penalty cases premised on "death is different" assumptions, despite that capital convicts represent but a tiny fraction of the mammoth prison population, which omits "99.999% of offenders from the protection of the Cruel and Unusual Punishments Clause." Hence, while the bulk of defendants are subject to seemingly endless imprisonment and solitary confinement, the Court, rather than watching the watchers, has had its eye on a different creature.

Chapter 14

How Mass Incarceration Underdevelops Latino Communities

In criminal justice scholarship, there is an abundance of research that charts the monumental growth of American prisons in the post–civil rights era. Scholars have labeled this punitive posture by a host of terms, perhaps most prominently mass incarceration or mass imprisonment. Other monikers include "hyper-incarceration," "warehousing," "prison industrial complex," and "incarceration nation." During this period, prison rates soared and in due time distinguished the country with the highest rate of incarceration and largest prison population in the world. The shift to incarceration, however, was not evenly spread among American society, but rather became the burden of underclass ethnic com- munities. While the darkening of American prisons has been well told, little research has focused on the implications for communities to which inmates return. Even less research focuses on Latino communities. This chapter contributes by offering a comprehensive picture of how the penal system not only arrests the development of Latino communities, but affirmatively works to hinder them.

Collateral Consequences: Shackles beyond the Sentence

Among the social effects of this situation is that communities are forced to absorb ever-increasing numbers of returning convicts, who return saddled not only by the stigma of imprisonment, but numerous collateral consequences that negatively affect the ex-felon and the entire community. The consequences are "collateral" as they arise from regulations of agencies outside the control of the justice system, which typically result in restrictions on housing, employment, licensing, and civic duties such as jury duty and voting. They are "not highly publicized" and represent "penalties, disabilities, or disadvantages" that occur automatically because of the conviction, in addition to the sentence itself.

In addition to the legal consequences, extralegal factors are critical to assessing the structural impacts on communities. These "invisible punishments" include policies and practices that, "overtly or subtly, advantage one racial group over another, thereby facilitating racially disparate outcomes" as well as other collateral consequences or "spillover" effects of imprisonment. For select communities, this comes with a hefty price, as they must reabsorb hundreds of thousands of inmates a year, including many who will return with various hardships and maladaptations that include post-traumatic stress disorders, physical and mental illness, addiction, and criminogenic proclivities such as rape and sexual assault. It is a losing situation for ex-prisoners since the communities to which they typically return are usually less stable and unable to provide social services.

Burdening Convicts and Their Communities

A felony conviction or time spent in prison is the scarlet letter of the present, which deeply impacts communities. A conviction leads to all sorts of social, political, and economic disadvantages for felons, and has been dubbed the "new civil death." In the aggregate, these obstacles make it difficult for released inmates to transition to society successfully, which, in turn, makes it difficult for these communities to achieve social stability. The pernicious effects are said to trigger a process of "intergenerational educational detainment," which increases risk of homelessness, inadequate health-care coverage, and disenfranchisement among the children of the incarcerated.

Imprisonment imposes economic hardships on both family and friends. The prisoner may be a parent, spouse, sibling, or other relative relied on by others, which makes the offender's family experience the incarceration as "de facto punishment." According to one study, family income is 22 percent lower after a father is incarcerated, while another showed that ex-prisoners earned wages 16–28 percent lower than the general population. Often, loved ones are sentenced vicariously, having to make long drives out to correctional facilities, expending personal and work-related time, gas, wear and tear on vehicles, and expenses for sending letters, packages, and money to commissary accounts, in addition to money for legal fees. In due course, "relatives find that providing money and other items for their imprisoned relatives is a byproduct of maintaining family contact."

Imprisonment strains relationships between inmates and family and friends. At a base social level are the shame and stigma of a relative's incarceration. Imprisonment is also associated with decreased marriage rates and high rates of divorce among the inner-city poor, the disruption of families, and growth in the prison population, which incurs "a large and unaccounted social cost." With divorce rates of about 50 percent, prisoners compare well to the population as a whole; however, it takes prisoners only a third of the time for their marriage to dissolve.

Long-term damage to the family is likely when the prisoner is a parent. Between adult and juvenile parents, there are currently over 2 million children in the United States with a parent currently serving time in prison; one quarter of all juveniles themselves have children, with Latino males constituting 20 percent of all parents in prison in 2007. Understanding the exact impact of having a parent incarcerated is complicated since the effect may be related to other competing hardships in a child's life, including "the parent-child separation, the crime and arrest that preceded incarceration, or the general instability and inadequate care at home." Nonetheless, the loss of a parent to prison is comparable to the way death or divorce impacts a child. Furthermore, removal and reentry of offenders impact some communities more than others, such that children are affected not only directly by incarceration in their home, but in the community at large. The effects are deleterious, and on average, children with a parent incarcerated are more likely to become delinquent themselves.

Educational gaps correlate with removal of a parent to prison, and the children of incarcerated parents are more likely to have school-related performance problems, depression, anxiety, and lower self-esteem. Increases in family disruption are associated with "increased risks of poor school performance by children, of domestic violence and of contact with the juvenile justice system." A mother's incarceration has been found to produce significant worsening of both reading scores and behavioral problems in affected children. One study reports that almost three out of five African American high-school dropouts will spend some time in prison. For felons, some of these educational deficiencies are traceable to government policies that disqualify felons from federal and state financial assistance. These factors contribute to school-to-prison pipelines, which are characterized as "policies and practices that push our nation's schoolchildren, especially our most at-risk children, out of classrooms and into the juvenile and criminal justice systems."

Broader consequences of imprisonment include increased prospects for crime and violence in communities. Even though the relationship among prisons, prisoner reentry, and crime is unclear, some studies have found that incarceration increases crime at the neighborhood level and beyond. More recent research indicates that increased incarceration is followed by increased crime.

The debilitating social effects are worsened by the political effect of felony disenfranchisement. As individual states determine voting and disenfranchisement laws, the great majority of states opt to disenfranchise felony convicts, a practice upheld as constitutional by the Supreme Court. Today, all but two states, Maine and Vermont, place some form of voting restrictions on convicted felons, while thirteen states and the District of Columbia prohibit convicted felons from voting only during imprisonment; thirty-five states extend disenfranchisement to probation, parole, or both, and in some states the restriction may be permanent.

Like the social and political consequences, imprisonment compromises the economic health of Latino communities. This is particularly so where state census policies permit the county in which a prisoner is held to claim the prisoner as a resident for state funding purposes. The practice diverts state funding from the home county of an offender to the county that holds the prisoner, effectively putting counties that house inmates in zero-sum resource competition with counties that supply them.

In some jurisdictions, the initial financial shock is the immediate order to pay a number of penalties associated with the crime. The variety of adverse consequence of legal debt on felons in states like Washington include "lost income, diminished occupational opportunities, depressed credit ratings, and heightened housing instability. Non-payment also has negative consequence for debtors including lost income (through garnishment), worsened credit ratings, prolonged court supervision, and issuance of an arrest warrant, which can trigger loss of social security benefits and even incarceration."

From Mass Incarceration to Mass Migrations

Upon release from prison, ex-felons may be civilly dead, but they nonetheless represent a living burden on their communities. This partly results from the many who return with substance abuse problems, including hard-drug addiction and alcoholism. According to the Bureau of Justice Statistics, most prisoners with abuse and addiction problems do not receive treatment while they are incarcerated. Unlike these badly needed services, drugs and homemade intoxicants are indeed available, which allows some ex-convicts to leave prison without substantial time in sobriety.

Returning convicts who are parents are also likely to encounter family difficulties upon reentry. For these individuals, there is little likelihood that they will be able to organize the lives of their children or exercise the decision-making responsibilities that parenting requires. For some, the issue is moot since a conviction may force a parent to forfeit custody rights or adoption rights altogether, or to terminate parental rights.

Finding a stable partner is difficult for ex-felons, since they are perceived as undesirable marriage partners. With few prospects for making a decent wage, diminished social status, and lack of self-esteem and resources, they are limited in appeal as a marriage partner, and young men in particular face reduced prospects for marriage. Further complicating prospects for successful partnerships is that some prisoners exit prison with a distorted sexual identity, which compromises healthy sexual intimacy outside of prison. The negative impacts on communities directly relate to the high rates of gender and sexual violence in prison. As criminologists have long maintained, men who are victimized by others in prison often leave the institution more violent and antisocial than when they entered. The quality of life back in the community is influenced by released prisoners who have experienced sexual violence, since they are more likely to become sexual offenders themselves. Prisons contribute through legal authorities, including staff and administrators, who routinely ignore constitutional, statutory, and institutional rules that obligate them to protect inmates against physical and sexual violence.

Communities that absorb large concentrations of released offenders are ultraburdened since they already struggle with high unemployment and a shortage of available jobs. The twin problem of being a felon and being in a surplus market coincides with the fact that every state restricts felons from certain jobs and professional licenses. According to one study, there are almost three hundred restricted jobs for felony convicts, which results in not just an economic penalty in the labor market, but a restriction to jobs characterized by high turnover and little upward mobility.

Even when an ex-prisoner succeeds in finding work, maintaining employment is an entirely different problem, one that is threatened when courts suspend an individual's driver's license. Despite the fact that the ability to drive may be essential to acquiring or keeping a job, in the state of Oregon it is standard practice for judges to suspend licenses for non-motor-vehicle-related crimes, such as failing to pay court fees and fines. The problem is circular, since the ability to pay these fines is largely a function of whether one can find work and transportation in the first place.

Under federal law, felony offenders are subject to an exclusive set of restrictions. For example, a federal felony conviction makes one ineligible to enlist in the armed forces, obtain federal employment, obtain a license to fly an aircraft, or obtain a private radio license, among other jobs and licenses. Moreover these professional disqualifications need not have a connection between the prior crime and the employment. For Latinos who are noncitizens, the severity reaches a zenith through deportation proceedings that may result from certain felony convictions.

Federal laws also ban felons from possessing a firearm. Although at face value, this may seem a reasonable policy, at times it sits in stark contrast to the security issues inmates face in the community. As described earlier, ex-felons are likely to return to places typified by higher rates of crime and violence, yet these individuals are barred from obtaining a firearm to protect themselves and their families. Although the right to bear arms is valued in American society and infuses the principles that underlie the "castle doctrine" and "stand your ground" laws, those most vulnerable in society are often the most defenseless, which is underscored by the fact that most prisoners are nonviolent offenders.

At the local level, ex-prisoners are ineligible for an array of social services, health benefits, or public housing. The bans in housing are somewhat superfluous since returning prisoners rarely have the financial resources or references to compete for housing in the private market. Prisoners typically must live with their family after release, which for some families in public housing is risky considering that illegal drug activity by the released individual puts the entire family at risk of eviction. This possibility raises the stakes for taking in a family member from prison, which are heightened considering the significant number of inmates who leave prison with substance abuse problems.

Mental health problems in prison generally increase exposure to these problems in communities through the release of ailing inmates. Even though prisons are the number one mental-health-care providers in this country by volume, mental illness is prevalent behind bars. Much of this development is the result of deinstitutionalization of the chronically mentally ill and the strong association of drug use, addiction, and mental illness that led the justice system to become the default mental-health response for the poor and homeless. Research has shown that mental illness is often needlessly triggered in prison through non- treatment, poor treatment, or disruptions in medication. In worst-case scenarios, excessive punishment in solitary confinement can produce permanent psychological damage. Moreover, released mentally ill offenders are likely to recidivate, which poses a unique threat to communities, since their inhabitants are the likely victims of the new crimes committed.

Prisoners also suffer from physical health problems, which become the community's problem as well. As prisoners have high rates of tuberculosis, and other sexually transmitted diseases, including syphilis and chlamydia, the ailments put home communities at high risk of exposure. HIV infection in the United States exemplifies the trends since prisoners are more than three times likely than the general population to be infected, with three-fourths of aids-related deaths being suffered by African Americans.

Scholars speculate that the high rates of HIV infection in prison are directly related to the rates found in Latino communities. Some have argued that War on Drugs policies and the subsequent incarceration of so many African American males were the principal causes of the increasing levels of HIV in African American communities. According to one scholar, drug use exposed significant numbers to HIV, while drug-related arrests and imprisonment that were part of the "War on Drugs" put large numbers of drug users—a group at great risk for infection—behind bars. This largely affected ethnic minorities, creating "the perfect engine for generating new infections and for disseminating the virus throughout the communities from which these men and women were taken." Another scholar offers a more race-based perspective, explaining that aids rates among white injection-drug users and their sexual partners are lower than Latino injection-drug users, because "drug use is treated as a public health problem when the user is white. White drug users are more likely to be sent to treatment centers than jail." Others have noted that forced sex in prison may be a contributing factor to the climbing rates of sexually transmitted diseases. The virus follows patterns of community concentration, and by 2006, three states accounted for 50 percent of known prison cases. Four years later, one researcher reported that upwards of 15,000 HIV-positive inmates are released from prison each year. Those who contract the virus in jails and prison bring it home to their family and others in the community.

The Justice System: Public Enemy No. 1 for Latino Communities

Latino communities are the destination for a disproportionate number of released prisoners, nearly three-fourths of whom come from impoverished ethnic communities. According to a study of relocation trends in Cleveland, Ohio, there is a presumption that returning prisoners are concentrated in the poorest neighborhoods. The vast majority of prisoners eventually exit prison and return to their old neighborhoods; yet according to another study, "ex-prisoners do not reenter communities randomly. They return to the communities from which they came or go to places that are very similar. Because the people who go to prison are overwhelmingly poor . . . they are drawn from and return to characteristically poor, ethnic neighborhoods."

Toward Arresting the Enemy

By now it is clear that for Latino communities, the justice system is public enemy number one, causing harm that has been described as "catastrophic" and "epidemic." With so many lives and communities wasting away, the situation calls for drastic actions to bring about a Great Reformation of mass incarceration. Although there is little doubt that some critics will deem these prescriptions as negligent or even dangerous, such a charge misses the point—that prisons are the most dangerous places in America, followed by the communities to which most prisoners return. Indeed, what is happening right now is dangerous: people are suffering, lives are being lost, families are being destroyed, and communities are crumbling. These realities provide a justification to "crash the system" that is so harmful to underclass communities.

Perhaps one of the most effective means of paralyzing the system would be for defendants to refuse to plea-bargain and instead exercise the right to a jury trial. The idea has been hypothesized by Michelle Alexander, who wonders, "What would happen if we organized thousands, even hundreds of thousands, of people charged with crimes to refuse to play the game, to refuse to plea out? What if they all insisted on their Sixth Amendment right to trial? Couldn't we bring the whole system to a halt just like that?" The question is grave in light of the fact that current plea-bargain regimes at the state level show that nearly 95 percent of cases are pled out of court, with some 96 percent of federal cases processed by plea bargain. These numbers suggest that if only a modest percentage of defendants refused to plea, it could create havoc in the courts.

Refusing to plea-bargain is a potent means for defendants to struggle against the system, yet civilians have powers at their disposal as well, particularly the power of jury nullification. Nullification occurs when a jury refuses to convict a defendant despite the prosecutor's success in proving all the elements of the crime. Jurors may annul the law collectively to achieve acquittals, or they may do so individually to yield hung juries and mistrials. Both are favorable for the defendant, since prosecutors are less likely to retry a mistrial. The power to nullify is ultimately a judicial check that gives the final say regarding punishment to twelve members of the community, above and beyond the interests of the state. At its foundation, the jury system afforded the most merciful leniency, since a judge could always set aside a conviction if the jury voted to convict, but if that jury voted to acquit, retrial was forbidden. The power of nullification underscores the importance of exercising the right to a jury trial, since nullification can be exercised in the trial setting only.

The strategies explored in this chapter, although not without controversy, may be the most immediately effective methods of combating the justice system's harsh impacts on Latino communities and beyond. Failure to stem the harm, however, should be even more controversial since it keeps Latino communities marching steadily on the path of underdevelopment.

Chapter 15

Facts and Fictions about Islam in Prison:
Assessing Prisoner Radicalization in Post-9/11 America

This chapter contributes to the discourse by analyzing how Islam impacts inmates by focusing on three primary objectives:

- Overviewing the political concerns about radicalization and highlighting factors that both promote and prevent it, as distilled from data on prisoners;

- Providing an account of Islamic outreach and its impact on inmates and prison culture;

- Positing that to the extent radicalization occurs in prisons, it has less to do with foreign influences and more the grievances about domestic matters, and American prisoners themselves are responsible for organizing subversive activity.

These findings reveal that radicalization to the point of adopting violence is a rare event. But to the extent that it does occur, it corresponds to concerns about the conditions of Muslims in the United States rather than to recruiting efforts launched by foreign networks in Muslim-majority countries. Although this latter hypothesis has proved irresistible for some, cases to date show that radicalization in prison has little to do with groups like al-Qaida, Saudi-based charities, or other foreign sources. This skewed view overlooks the great deal of fuel for radicalization that prisoners find at home, including racism and religious discrimination, which bear more on an inmate's thinking. Moreover, inmates themselves are the single most important factor for the spread of extremism. As one researcher states: "die-hard extremists need little proselytizing from Wahhabi clerics from abroad. They are already prison radicals of the first order, many of whom are fully capable of radicalizing other inmates on their own." The influence of these already radicalized inmates is magnified by policies that restrict Islamic religious leaders from entering prisons and a de facto hiring freeze at the federal level. These distinctions are key to understanding how extremism spreads and how penal policies contribute to the problem.

CONCLUSIONS

False Alarms: Extremist Violence in Prison and Foreign Recruitment

One immediate starting point is for elected officials and some researchers to use better, more precise terminology. Those engaged in the debate need to make a constitutional distinction between thought and actual criminal behavior. Employing radicalization as a catchall term is not only contrary to our nation's values, but it also sets the basis for poor security policies that opt to scrutinize beliefs subjectively, rather than objectively identify dangerous behaviors.

There is also greater need for further research on Islam in prisons that uses standard social science methodologies and is conducted by teams of interdisciplinary scholars. The discussions distilled from past congressional hearings further highlight this need, not to mention that basic information about Islam in prison is still unknown by many of those who conduct such hearings, including conversion rates or how many Muslims are currently incarcerated. These blind spots testify to the need for more systematic data collection and analysis. To move these efforts forward, Muslim communities have played an integral role in supporting research and scholarly endeavors. But what is required now is additional support from other sectors. Whether this comes via institutional support in the form of Islamic studies departments in colleges and universities, think tanks, or seminary training for inmates who want to become imams, the resulting long-term investment is a social good. Not only will it lay down an academic foundation for Islamic history and knowledge in this country, but the creation of knowledge will also contribute to better cultural understanding among Muslims, as well as between Muslims and non-Muslims. To facilitate research endeavors, the report recommends that such civil society and government agencies as the national institute for Justice and the office of community-oriented Policing services support more research by arranging conferences and grants in the following areas:

- The effectiveness of faith-based, and specifically Islamic, outreach programs for incarcerated and released offenders;

162

- Nationwide studies of prisoner recidivism rates that track religion and reflect the commission of new crimes, rather than technical parole violations;

- The needs of released inmates, including evidence-based programs that seek to reduce violence, crime, and extremism inside prisons;

- The development and implementation of better gang intelligence detection procedures and infrastructure at state-run facilities nationwide; and

- The development and implementation of uniform vetting and supervision procedures for religious workers at state-run facilities nationwide.

The need for more serious efforts at objective research is particularly crucial for the government, because its absence has resulted in uninformed federal policies. indeed, some researchers note that the government has lagged behind the research efforts of other countries: "in light of the powerful emotions that are provoked by the fear of prison radicalization, the failure to move ahead with that kind of research effort will mean that policy will inevitably be carried along not by reason, but by the political passions inevitably at play."

Toward Best Practices

The lack of evidence supporting claims of violent extremism among Muslim inmates leads to telling conclusions, one of them being that there have been more congressional hearings in the last decade on extremist violence than actual instances of Muslim inmates engaging in religious terrorism. Recent research supports the point, noting that "much of the talk about the risk of radicalization is simply talk, unsupported by research or evidence." Equally telling is the little that has been said about prison converts who have helped foil terrorist plots, such as the case of Derrick Shareef, who planned to attack a shopping mall but was stopped by the FBI with the help of ex-gang member and prison convert William "Jamaal" Chrisman. Chrisman stated that he decided to work as an informant to help the government after 9/11, because "scholars in Saudi Arabia and morocco said that it was incumbent on Muslims to stop terrorists." This theme was echoed in the 2011 Seattle terrorist plot, which was also foiled with the help of a prison convert. These countervailing narratives of extremism are absent from the discourse, and yet the fact remains: although there is only one conclusive case of prison-based terrorism, there are at least two cases of prison converts working with officials to help foil terrorist attacks.

The relative rarity of violent extremism involving Muslim inmates is noteworthy for policymakers, since it suggests that radicalization is better approached through preventative strategies than through more forceful intervention. As one study has declared: "the current claims that prison radicalization has reached a crisis stage are grossly premature and, at this point, mere speculation." Although some prison systems have adopted suppressive "counter" strategies, these approaches, including restricting imams, books, and even communications, has become the norm in some institutions, despite that such tactics run the risk of backfiring and fomenting radicalism or, as the same study warned, "hysteric and stigmatizing reaction can fuel radicalization among prisoners and their followers, contributing to the threat rather than managing it." British prison officials have been learning this lesson, since their extreme security measures have inspired greater resistance among radicals. More importantly, the attempt to shape religious ideology by censorship or otherwise is dangerous and instead may stoke animosity and fear. The final pages of this chapter consider ways to advance the discussion and reduce the potential for extremist violence through fostering a diverse marketplace of Islamic ideas, reforming institutional policies, improving training for staff, and stabilizing prisoner re-entry.

Fostering an Islamic Marketplace

Since prison-based extremist violence has yet to manifest itself in any meaningful way, policymakers should develop and implement proactive strategies to help maintain the status quo. There are now, more than ever, good reasons to adopt preventative approaches: the unprecedented scale of imprisonment and the fact that increasing numbers of inmates will be released with each passing year. Ultimately, this strategy requires deep structural changes, and primarily, would direct prevention efforts at those institutional factors that feed into radicalization, particularly the lack of viable leadership and overcrowding.

Although representative Peter King has publicly stated his intention "to stop prisoners from being radicalized," his ability to do so would be highly unlikely even in the best-functioning prison systems. Given the significant internal administrative challenges and the external social, political, and economic issues, calling for a complete halt to radicalization is simply unrealistic, not to mention unconstitutional. But this is not to say that one should ignore the issue. Rather, it requires a balanced approach; one that neither underestimates nor overestimates the challenges, is the most prudent way forward. As such, it is necessary to understand the separate but related issues of extremist ideology and extremist violent crime. Parsing these challenges will provide policymakers, correctional practitioners, and community stakeholders with a better way to develop proactive and effective strategies for public safety.

An unbalanced approach yields such failed policies as the BOP standardized chapel library Project, which sought to inventory all current holdings and determine their permissibility under the BOP's security policies. This project offers a compelling example of how suppressive tactics can backfire and antagonize Muslim inmates, rather than reduce radicalization. The subsequent removal of texts was reported to have greatly frustrated inmates, some of whom had been reading a particular book for decades but were now told that it was off-limits. From their perspective, this policy was paternalistic and may have also overlooked how such literature may help counter extremism and thus produce a normalizing effect by acting as a repellant, similar to how the great majority of non-imprisoned Muslims are averse to extremism. This harmful strategy also potentially hinders the more effective monitoring of inmates. as one panelist at the 2011 hearings noted, "if an individual in a correctional institution possesses these types of radical material, it's actually, in a way, an investigative benefit because that person is then self-identifying as someone that bears further inspection and someone that can be monitored by the correctional staff."

There are better and more systematic approaches to preventing extremist violence. One is to foster a more diverse marketplace of ideas within state and federal prison systems in order to achieve a pluralistic religious environment. Achieving such a result involves generation of a multiplicity of religious views and options, as well as facilitating the entry of a more diverse body of Islamic leaders to administer programs. Practically, this might be carried out by any number of means, such as broadcasting live prayer services on closed circuit television or offering Arabic classes. Such measures should be adopted in recognition of Islam as a rather complex religion, and that adopting any singular approach to it is not only dangerous ideologically, but also contrary to religious life on the ground. Fostering a marketplace is the opposite of trying to establish what one scholar has dubbed "official Islam," or a government-sponsored account of Islam.

Prison officials and policymakers should take the following steps to promote pluralism:

> 1. Lower barriers for religious leaders to enter. BOP officials should reassess their ban on hiring Muslim prison chaplains from such endorsing agencies as the Islamic society of North America (ISNA). Statements made against them lack factual basis and are mostly promoted by unreliable sources advocating an anti-Muslim agenda. Despite the allegations against ISNA, a 2005 senate investigation cleared it and other organizations of any wrongdoing. Additionally, the BOP has made extensive use of contracted religious service providers, a policy that has not effectively addressed inmates' present or long-term needs. The lack of Muslim religious leaders must be remedied, so that trained religious leaders become the rule instead of the exception. In the Pew survey of state prison chaplains, 55% of participants agreed that Islam is the faith group with the greatest need for more volunteers, while 83% believed that Christian faith groups have "more than necessary." Such statistics feed into the claim that radicalization occurs when prisons "promote Christianity and starve Islam." state correctional institutions implementing similar bans or severe restrictions should also reassess or, where applicable, develop policies that strike an adequate balance between vetting and providing services.

> 2. Professionalize Islamic chaplaincy. Prison administrators should make greater efforts to hire and retain qualified imams who have been certified by prison authorities or through religious training. This would take Islamic leadership in a more authentic direction, as according to one leading criminologist, "a

minimum standard of theological education" can help avert the schooling of extremists in prison.

3   Encouraging religious "entrepreneurship." Prison officials and policymakers should be urged to continue engaging with a wide variety of Muslim faith-based organizations. This includes increasing access to various types of religious texts and religious workers who adhere to differing interpretations of Islam. the Ohio department of corrections has established a framework for faith-based engagement and a "best practices" tool-kit for faith-based programming.185 Prisons with large Muslim populations should implement an Islamic studies certification program to increase basic religious literacy. To go one step further, they should create a pool of potential Islamic leaders. One model to consider may be California's Folsom state Prison's Islamic studies Program, which has reportedly helped inmate rehabilitation. To avoid any potential state endorsement of religion and to ensure quality control of the curriculum, such a program could be done in partnership with an officially accredited academic institution (e.g., a seminary or a theological studies department at a college or university). Here, the Saint Louis University Prison Program is instructive, since it began by offering inmates a certificate in theological studies. Over time, it expanded to offer inmates and staff the opportunity to earn an associate's degree. Corrections officials would be wise to provide staff with basic religious competency training and recruiting more Muslim staff for prisons with significant Muslim populations. Such basic religious sensitivity training and proactive recruitment would contribute more "cultural and political capital" by adding legitimate and moderate voices of religious authority, as well as promote goodwill and increase the Muslim inmates' respect for prison administration officials. The resulting knowledge gained could help identify extremism as well as avoid unnecessary confrontation with prisoners, such as those that triggered the 1993 Lucasville riot.

Prison administrations should provide adequate worship space for different Muslim subgroups. In recent years, Sunni inmates have sued to have services held separately from those of Shia inmates and vice versa, even though the courts remain unreceptive to the idea. In practice, this position overlooks important sectarian differences. As neither sect is recognized as authoritative enough to warrant its own space for worship, there is a greater likelihood of mutual rivalry and antagonism. Although prison authorities have cited security reasons for denying this request, it is precisely because of security concerns, namely, sectarian tensions flaring into violence, that administrators should reconsider their positions, lest these concerns become a self-fulfilling prophecy. As Kevin Lamar James' case revealed, animosity toward other religious groups goes right to the heart of legitimacy, which current policies discount by not affording separate spaces.

Stabilizing Prisoner Re-Entry

Prisons should implement more effective methods of reintegrating released prisoners into society, which is commonly referred to as "re-entry." As it stands, the more than 700,000 inmates released each year often do not get far beyond the prison gates before they experience the vacuum left by communities, government, and a general lack of support. As Frank Cillufo, director of the Homeland security Policy institute at George Washington university attests: "Former inmates are vulnerable to radicalization and recruitment because many leave prison with very little financial or social support. Similarly, others have stressed the importance of "after care" and policy measures that seek to facilitate this transition into a stable environment and make them less susceptible to recruitment by extremists. Accordingly, researchers explain that the "moment of release" presents an opportunity for policy innovations to develop bridges during the ensuing transition period. Yet if services are not forthcoming, a void is left open for gangs and other extremists. By helping prisoners get through this time of greatest need, radical groups build upon the loyalty developed in prison or afterwards, which is also a tactic of gangs and white supremacist groups. In this regard, one might reconsider Padilla and Reid as poster boys for unsuccessful re-entry rather than for prison-based extremism. As one study notes that, "If anything, these cases are a good illustration of why the systematic provision of after-care is so critical." Of the chaplains asked about this particular point, 78% of them stated that support from religious groups after release is one of the most critical factors for an inmate's successful re-entry. Administrators should implement re-entry services as an integral part of the corrections process with the following goals as guidance:

Connect re-entry to education on the inside and the outside. Re-entry programs should involve educational training on the inside and focus on educational opportunities to continue studying on the outside. Education increases rehabilitation and reduces recidivism, both of which directly impact extremism, for al-Qaida and similar groups prey on uneducated and economically desperate individuals. Education as a counter-balance to radicalization should therefore be a focal point of any prevention effort.

Ensure that all inmates receive re-entry services. As their release date approaches, inmates should receive, at a minimum, basic services such as obtaining a driver's license, a birth certificate, and a social security card, as well as outpatient mental health care services, if needed. Prison and criminal justice officials should explore possible public-private partnerships to improve service provisions and share the financial and material costs.

Explore ways to parole inmates into stable religious communities. Although this may be challenging, there is already an intensive outreach effort among African-American mosques and some partnerships are being established. Prison administrators should consider building on this model and seek to raise funds through faith-based initiatives. Devising ways to improve the situation of Muslim inmates is not the sole duty of criminal justice officials. Muslim communities and society at large have a significant stake in this matter and thus are partially obligated to help combat radicalization. Communities, which are victimized by acts of religious violence, must take the lead in quelling extremism. According to one report, some have already done so: "The Muslim community has been extremely active in combating terrorism, particularly with partnerships with law enforcement." Like the prison converts mentioned above, these communities have helped foil terrorist plots and remain a force for moderation. They should support other long-term strategies, such as:

Investing in efforts that will ensure the education and development of a long-term indigenous religious leadership. Even without the BOP's hiring freeze, it is likely that state and federal prisons will continue to experience shortages of professional Muslim religious workers and clergy given the lack of professional training and accrediting organizations. Communities must continue to support existing institutions and support the development of new ones.

Encouraging information sharing as regards chaplains. This is especially important where immigrant-origin American Muslim chaplains seek to guide mostly African-American prison congregations. as one African-American Muslim chaplain pointed out, an immigrant chaplain who is unaware of how Islam has developed among African-Americans is likely to quickly run into conflict and lose the inmates' respect as well as any credibility that he might have acquired. It is recommended that briefing materials and other resources be available to all chaplains so that they can familiarize themselves with the full diversity of this country's Muslim community, including those behind bars.

Encouraging intra-faith dialogue. Although Muslims have been involved in interfaith dialogue with Jews, Christians,

Hindus, and other religious groups, there has been little dialogue among themselves. Such dialogues, however, benefit all parties involved and are particularly important for Muslims, given that their various internal divides have proved somewhat artificial. With a significant number of Sunni Muslims having received their first start in nationalist understandings of Islam, the groups are less opposed than might be imagined. Instead, they might be better understood as being in a symbiotic relationship with the marginal groups that primes and prepares them to transition to more normative forms. At the very least, this decades-old trend offers common ground for discussion.

Increasing the social services infrastructure. After their release, many of these Muslims need considerable help in finding a job and a temporary place to live, as well as in accessing mental or physical clinical services. unfortunately, some preliminary evidence from new York and Indiana indicates that Islamic organizations are not doing enough to help them. in general, the united states has witnessed unprecedented numbers of released inmates returning to communities that are less stable and less able to provide the social services that inmates need to re-enter society. This is largely due to cultural resistance, as well as a lack of funds in many of those urban areas that need services the most. Local communities, particularly those with more resources and funds, must continue to help poorer communities build the necessary infrastructure that will help rehabilitate parolees. Indeed, former prisoners are often at a double disadvantage: they return to communities already struggling with high rates of poverty and unemployment, and they themselves are burdened with the stigma of criminal conviction and a lack of vocationaltraining.

Lower barriers to re-entry. In general, the nation needs to reform its criminal justice policy. Re-entering society is so difficult because it has been made that way through a host of restrictions, including those on voting, welfare services, housing, employment, driving and professional licensing. Each of these restrictions can, in some small way, guarantee failure. These civil barriers push the released prisoners back into a life of crime and render them more susceptible to recruitment by extremists. The final takeaway is that we must either adopt policies that seek to help these ex-prisoners or suffer the consequences of allowing others to do so.

These strategies are useful particularly because they impact more than just Muslim inmates; they help the whole inmate population and individuals and families on the outside as well. Supporting a more pluralistic environment is an overall good, for it gives insight into managing other religious groups. Likewise, stabilizing re-entry is important not just for preventing extremism among Muslims, but across all groups, since most released prisoners face the same obstacles. In the coming years, prisons will be releasing more inmates than any other time in this country's history. This fact makes the implementation of more effective policies all the more urgent.

Chapter 16

Spectacular or Specious?
A Critical Review of The Spectacular Few: Prisoner Radicalization and the Evolving Terrorist Threat

Debates about the role American prisons play in "homegrown" or domestic terrorism grow with each passing year. However, much of the debate has been premised on alarmist rationales, political distortions, and faulty analyses. The book, *The Spectacular Few: Prisoner Radicalization and the Evolving Terrorist Threat* by criminologist Mark Hamm is an attempt to assess the situation in the United States. As this book represents the first to tackle the question of prisoner radicalization, it is important by its great potential to influence scholarship, law, and policy. What follows offers a critique of the book's main thesis, which posits that prison conditions are the main cause of prisoner radicalization. It scrutinizes the methods and samples used to substantiate this and other claims. The critique shows how lack of rigorous analysis can lead to unfounded beliefs, including that prisons are breeding grounds for jihadist recruitment. A proper review of the book's successes and failures helps clarify key concepts and the scope of the problem, and hopefully, lead to better policies and greater justice in prison.

INTRODUCTION TO THE TOPIC

In post-9/11 America, concerns and fears about Islamic radicalization grow with each passing year. American prisons are no exception, and they too have become the center of debate, with some describing prisons as "fertile soil for jihad" or "breeding grounds" for al-Qaeda. These bold pronouncements, however, have not manifested in any meaningful way among state or federal prisoners, and instead sit in tension with life on the ground. As one researcher reported in 2013, since 2001, there has been only one case of homegrown jihadist violence involving inmates. Furthermore, ethnographic research shows radicalization among Muslim prisoners as deeply rooted in domestic grievances. Disaffection is not the sign of successes in foreign proselytization, but about systemic unfairness at home, including in criminal justice, racial and religious oppression, and anti-Muslim policy abroad.

Academic inquiry into the question of prisoner radicalization has yielded mixed results. This area of study suffers its share of problems, with lack of rigor and methodological problems being duly noted. More basically, determining what exactly is meant by "radicalization" has proved critical, and "the inability of scholars, politicians, chaplains, and even prisoners themselves to devise a common definition of radicalization means that it is extremely difficult to develop any model that explains why it occurs."

Arguably, the most difficult issue in trying to understand prisoner radicalization is causality. Determining the factors that coalesce to motivate an individual to adopt extreme beliefs and behaviors is especially difficult since some inmates have extremist inclinations well before they are imprisoned. Determining the prison's role is thus no easy task when individuals enter prison with clearly extremist views, agendas, and proclivities. For these individuals, imprisonment is merely a pit stop on a journey that started well before entering the prison gates. Others, on the contrary, may not participate in extremist activities until years after their release from prison. In both cases, the prison's role may be far from certain, yet both caution against turning a radical into a case of "prisoner radicalization" just because of time spent in prison.

THE BOOK: THESIS, METHOD, AND COROLLARY ARGUMENTS

In *The Spectacular Few: Prisoner Radicalization and the Evolving Terrorist Threat*, criminologist Mark Hamm uses ethnographic data to explore the topic of prisoner radicalization. The book's central argument holds that harsh prison conditions are at the root of inmate radicalization. Radicals are created by overcrowded conditions and violent penal regimes, including the threat of physical and psychological violence, gang activity, and other deprivations of imprisonment. These are the factors that Hamm believes lead inmates to adopt extremist ideology, violence, and terrorism. From this perspective, the common denominator for inmates who embark on this path is their prison experience.

Hamm introduces the reader to the topic through short vignettes of what he calls the "invisible history" of prisoner radicalization. According to the author, this history is invisible because prisoner radicalization has always been a part of world history, even though it may not be well known. To make this history visible, he offers up Winston Churchill,

Mahatma Gandhi, Nelson Mandela, and Adolf Hitler as an initial set of case studies in prisoner radicalization.

Beginning with Winston Churchill, the author describes Churchill's journey to cover a war in South Africa in the hopes of jump-starting his career in journalism. In his quest, Churchill was arrested and held in a South African detention facility. After spending a few months there, he escaped and returned to Britain. Later, in his autobiography, Churchill recalls his experience in the prison camp: "We had so much liberty in our bounds, and were so free from observation during the greater part of the day and night." He also recounts that when he made his escape, he wore a civilian suit, and had 75 British pounds in his pocket, along with slabs of chocolate. He would later claim to have hated this period more than any other in his life.

The next example is Mahatma Gandhi, whom the author notes, was imprisoned for "nonviolent civil disobedience campaigns." These campaigns against the British government involved breaking laws through nonviolence, "thereby forcing the British to punish protestors with brutal physical beatings and imprisonment." During his incarceration, Gandhi used time to his advantage, as "unlimited time to read, write, meditate and organize," and as one of Gandhi's biographers describes, "prison never held any terrors for him." Indeed, he was in and out of jail several times, and on various occasions took vows to fast until death.

Hamm's next prisoner radicalization prototype is Nelson Mandela, who spent nearly three decades incarcerated in apartheid South Africa. According to the author, Mandela first entered prison with an already rebellious attitude, and was "as uncooperative" as he could be from his first day of imprisonment. From that day on, as with Gandhi, Mandela passed his time in prison under a "personal campaign of reading, writing, and organizing."

The book's last example points to the "dark side" of prisoner radicalization in the person of Adolf Hitler. Imprisoned in Germany for high treason, Hitler was held in a facility where he received favorable treatment from both guards and staff who sympathized with his plight. As a prisoner, Hitler was permitted all sorts of accommodations, including mounds of gifts and clothing, visitors, and even a personal servant and chauffer. He had no restrictions placed on correspondence or reading privileges and he was able to establish personal relationships with future Reich leaders. During this time he also began composition of the celebrated and despised *Mein Kampf*, which lays out a global plan of genocide against Jewish people. In total, Hitler spent nine months in prison, which according to the author, was when he "refined his strategy to gain power and elevated his self-belief through the Fuhrer."

These stories set the stage for the next part of the book, which explores Islam's early history in American prisons up to the 1960s. Specifically citing Folsom Prison and its "long and storied radical history . . . ," the example advances a key piece of the book's thesis that the prison environment itself is the primary factor for catalyzing radicalism.

TEXTUAL ANALYSIS: SHORTCOMINGS AND STRENGTHS

Academic Shortcomings: The Devil's in the Details

Perhaps the greatest difficulty of this work is its tendency to undermine its own thesis, namely, that "prisoner radicalization occurs only under specific conditions of confinement." The problem with this view is exemplified in the very case studies given in the book, which are worth reexamining in hindsight in light of the author's main argument.

Churchill fares poorly as an example of prison radicalization. His story tells of an individual who, for the sake of jump-starting his career, went to a warring country. The story lends itself to the idea that Churchill had extreme ways well before his prison experience. Even granting that he had no radical proclivities prior to his captivity, his imprisonment hardly describes the type of prison that causes inmates to radicalize. One need only recall that Churchill enjoyed "so much liberty" and was "free from observation for most of the day." This was not Foucault's panopticon, but a place that he could escape well-dressed with cash and chocolate. The depiction of Churchill as a prison radical seemingly falls flat.

The cases of Gandhi and Mandela are less convincing still. Again, looking at their biography, it is no stretch to suggest that both of these individuals were radicals *well before they entered prison*. As Hamm mentions, Gandhi had already gone on hunger fasts to protest treatment of the untouchables and was deeply involved in organizing widespread law-breaking through non-violent tactics. Moreover, his confinement was not under the harsh, brutal confines that foment radicalization. Instead, it was a place for "unlimited time to read, write, meditate, and organize."

Like Gandhi, Mandela's case bears no indicators of the thesis. In fact his biography may perhaps be best viewed as an antithesis of sorts. For example, although the book omits the point, Mandela was sentenced to imprisonment as a result of his campaigns to bomb government targets.

At that time he believed in violence as a means to achieve political results, an attitude that was well formed by the time he entered prison such that he was as uncooperative as possible, *from his very first day*. Even then, the prison became a place for him to continue his political work until he was eventually released and would go on to became the president of South Africa and a Noble Peace Prize winner. Ironically, in this example, imprisonment, rather than produce a violent extremist, may have helped turn a violent extremist into a pacifist.

Of all the examples, Adolf Hitler is the most suspect of all. As the author himself describes, Hitler entered prison with a vehement hatred for anything Jewish. Accordingly, during his nine-month stay, Hitler began working on a book that outlined his genocidal policy to rid the world of Jews. In addition, his stay in prison can hardly be described as oppressive or harsh, rather, he enjoyed roomfuls of gifts and had many frequent visitors. Hitler's time in prison was unlike the typical Big House experience, and there is little evidence to support that his imprisonment had a radicalizing effect on his views. For as the record shows, these were set long before, and continued long after, his stay in prison. For Hitler, imprisonment appears as an incidental stop on a path of extremism.

According to the author, three of the four individuals exited prison without ever engaging in violence. Only one, Hitler, the least convincing of the examples, went on to orchestrate violence after his stay in prison. As an initial matter, then, the book's introduction turns out to be a smokescreen of examples that undermine the book's core thesis. Instead of igniting radicalism with dangerous, overcrowded, and chaotic environments, imprisonment offered them opportunity to develop radical agendas that were already in progress.

These red herrings go undetected by the reader in part because the introduction offers no definition of what is meant by "radicalization." This assessment can only be ascertained later since the reader is not given a definition until two chapters later where the author writes, "In the United States, prisoner radicalization is defined as the 'process by which inmates adopt extreme views, including beliefs that violent measures need to be taken for political or religious purposes.'" This definition is obviously problematic, but it also begs important questions, like "who" in the United States defines it this way? Also, is the definition sound? Are there contestations of it? More critically, how can the author adopt this definition *now*? Now, meaning after haven given the examples Churchill, Gandhi, Mandela, and Hitler.

The author's subsequent adoption of this definition and the examples amounts to a classic bait-and-switch. It baits the reader with examples of prisoner radicalization that end up not being examples under the author's adopted definition. The switch occurs by the book's nearly exclusive focus on Muslims; it goes from focusing on non-Muslim examples to focusing on Muslims for practically the rest of the book. In this sequence, case studies about non-Muslims who turn out to be peacemakers, get turned inside out since the rest of the text focuses entirely on Muslim prisoners who espouse violence.

These problems arise primarily because of the work's lack of discipline and design. The problem is compound—lack of a theoretical framework to understand the issue as well as failure to delimit the scope of study. The work offers no map of the academic terrain: cases of prisoner radicalization are stripped from their history and context, there are no geographical limits, and the evidence marshaled comes from all corners.

Moreover, the book falls into the trap of conflating "radicalization" and "conversion." As the book's preface notes, a report by the Senate Foreign Relations Committee claims that thirty-six Americans had converted to Islam while incarcerated in the United States and had traveled to Yemen to study Arabic. The author quotes the report, reiterating that these "radicalized ex-prisoners" may have gone to get training from al-Qaeda fighters. Although the report turns the converts into "radicalized ex- prisoners," nowhere does the author step in with a corrective. The repetition of the error transforms an innocuous event into something more menacing and makes every convert to Islam a potential threat.

In the JIS case it is clear that inmates participated in a conspiracy to attack American targets, although it is far from clear whether the case can be understood as an example of "prisoner radicalization," as the book has it. To be certain, by the time the mastermind behind the plot, Kevin James, stepped behind prison walls, he "liked to carry guns and steal," and prior to his most recent arrest, James had been in and out of juvenile and adult facilities, was active in a criminal street gang, and was convicted of robbery. In the span of his life, the prison appears as nothing more than a stop for a life characterized by extremist and risk-laden behavior. Hence, even though James is portrayed as a concrete example of prisoner radicalization, this says little about behavior that manifested before prison.

More directly to the work's thesis, there is little to suggest that prison conditions had anything to do with James' terrorist goals. Some researchers have even posited that conditions of confinement *likely did not* play a significant role in the plots, instead suggesting that James was more interested in dealing with enemies like the Nation of Islam and

Shia Muslims than prison guards. They also point out that his 100-page manifesto gives no indication of grievances with guards or the prison institution, which seemingly suggests, "if bad prison conditions or the humiliation of the prison experience had moved James toward radicalization, then it is reasonable to expect that he would have said so in this document. Yet, he did not. That James's manifesto did not dwell on prison conditions suggests other reasons for his radicalization." Despite these challenges, Hamm dismisses the critiques as counterfactuals, which, he writes, are "treated with amusement by the intelligence community."

Nonetheless, it hardly taxes the imagination to suggest that people like James are likely to continue with violent behavior after incarceration—only a cursory understanding of his personal history would render his actions "spectacular"—more soberly, they are exactly what one might expect from him.

Formulating Fiction: Failed Foreign-Invasion Hypothesis

Another area of weakness is the work's tendency to perpetuate misunderstandings about Islam in prison. Perhaps most prominent is the idea that U.S. prisons are a fifth column for international terror networks like al-Qaeda. Even though the author separates himself from the "alarmist camp," as he deems it, he constantly indicates that American prisoners have "ties" or "links" to foreign organizations. Although such words can encompass the most distant relationships, it is not clear what a "link" actually is or what it means to have "ties." On this point, the author gives no guidance.

A few examples of this orientation make the point. Already discussed are the three dozen prison-converts who, it was speculated, may have gone to the Middle East to collaborate with al-Qaeda. There is also the opening narrative of the book that described an ex-detainee from Guantanamo who was involved in the "Christmas Day" plot in 2009. With no empirical support, Hamm states that this individual was "radicalized in a U.S. operated prison. For support, he proffers a statement from the inmate's family, who attribute his extremism to the five years he spent at Guantanamo Bay. A report by the Department of Defense, however, stated that this individual had spent two months in Afghanistan in military training facility *before* his capture by U.S. forces. Hamm's treatment of this individual as an example of prisoner radicalization is not only specious, but it also furthers the idea that al-Qaeda holds influence over American prisoners. As he writes, "while Islam is mainly a positive influence in prison, certain forces within the prison Muslim

SpearIt

movement are aligned with the efforts of al-Qaeda and its associates to inspire convicts in the United States and Europe to conduct terrorist attacks on their own."

Such claims, however, have been debunked, as acknowledged by Hamm himself in a 2009 article that cites a study in which the FBI conducted over 2,088 terrorism threat assessments in prisons and jails across the United States and "determined there was *not* a JIS-like pattern of terrorist recruitment in US prisons . . . Indeed, the FBI could find no pattern of terrorist recruitment whatsoever." Nonetheless Hamm adheres to the JIS as an iteration of al-Qaeda's influence. With no positive evidence that this organization or its members had communications or connections with foreign terrorist organizations, the author asserts, "The JIS plot was part of an international post-9/11 trend toward homegrown terrorist cells whose members tend to seek al-Qaeda's blessing."

Taken wholly, *The Spectacular Few: Prisoner Radicalization and the Evolving Terrorist Threat* is as specious as it is speculative. When the book is distilled to its essence, it can claim one concrete example of a Muslim group, the JIS case, "Al-Qaeda of California," which involved inmates in a terrorist plot—even though it is still unclear whether the prison catalyzed any of the violent plans. Furthermore, to date, there is still no example of a group involving prisoners that has actually attempted a terrorist attack. Although the book would have the reader believe that prisons are fertile fields for growing jihadists, the landscape is relatively bare.

Even then, the JIS case itself is hardly spectacular and should not be made into more than it is. The facts of the case are far more mundane than the author leads the reader to believe; this was a group that had no military training, no international associates, and no money. Its members were hardly skilled criminals—in fact the beginning of the end of their "fully operational" plot was foiled when a cohort outside of prison left his cell phone at the site where he had committed a robbery. Their follies and foibles hardly bring the word "spectacular" to mind.

Moreover, many of the claims made in the work go unsubstantiated either by primary or secondary sources, the results of which are many unsupported statements. Consider the assertion in the preface: "Islam is now sweeping across Western prisons, bringing with it . . . unprecedented security challenges." What sense should be made of such a claim? After all, in the United States, conversion to Islam is nothing new in prisons, and scholars have noted the religion's positive impacts since at least the 1960s. Since those days, Islamic outreach has evolved into the most sophisticated and well-organized missionary force in

180

prison. There is nothing "sweeping" about this—it is the product of decades of focused prison ministry rather than a post-9/11 fad.

It is likewise a stretch to contend that any sort of "sweeping" is going on in European prisons. For example, in Britain, the prison population is nearly 8% Asian, a significant portion of which is Muslims from Pakistan and India. This population, along with foreign nationals, helps to account for a higher percentage of Muslims in prison, not widespread proselytization. In France, although Muslims represent only about 12% of the civilian population, they make up over 60% of prisoners. These figures are not pretensions of widespread conversion behind bars as much as disproportional arrest and conviction of Muslims in the first place. The same holds true in the Netherlands and Belgium, who have Muslim populations from Morocco and Turkey that make up 16% of the prison population compared to less than 2% of the general population. For the author to claim that Islam is "sweeping across Western prisons" is inaccurate at best, for as these figures show, it may be more accurate to say that in Europe, Muslims are being swept *into* prisons.

Finally, although the book never explicitly states that it is a study on Islam, it devotes the lion's share of attention to Muslim prisoners. The end result is a work that begins with non-examples of prisoner radicalization that lead to discussions about Muslims, where other non-examples are given, ultimately leading to discussions of al-Qaeda. These imaginative constructs, however, say little about the fact that prison gangs and white supremacist groups are the greatest threat to both prison and national security

Strengths: Calling Attention to Prison Conditions & Showcasing the Need for Interdisciplinary Study

Perhaps the greatest contribution of this book is in calling attention to prison conditions and the treatment of prisoners in America. Although the author takes too far the argument that prisoner radicalization manifests as a result of the prison experience alone, it is without a doubt that conditions contribute to radicalization among all types of inmates, not only Muslims. In this regard, the author is to be commended by highlighting the fact that the government plays a significant role in the process.

As *The Spectacular Few* represents the first book on the topic of Muslim radicalization in prison, it exemplifies why interdisciplinary collaboration is the best approach to complex issues like prisoner radicalization. The book, despite its proclamation of being an

SpearIt

ethnographic work, presents little primary research. There are few narratives about inmates or testimony from incarcerated Muslims, and there is little detail about the method for acquiring and interpreting the data.

The most poignant example is the author's treatment of the JIS case. For example, in order to illustrate the "JIS Recruitment Strategy," the book contains a circular diagram that begins with "traditional American Islam," which leads to "pious prison Islam," then "prison gang," "street gang," and onto "international jihad movement," culminating in "terrorist plot." With little explanation as to how this sequence was devised or how the data support the diagram, the ultimate arrival to "international jihad movement" appears speculative more than spectacular. This is particularly so when remembering that the JIS had no international relationships—they were completely on their own. The diagram effectively turns a group of bumbling criminals into something far more ominous.

A study of such sensitive topics demands more rigorous analysis of the ethnography, as well as the religious aspects. Although the author claims the work is grounded in ethnography, there is little indication of collaboration or even citation of scholars or methods in this field. Moreover, there is little mention of the classic or cutting-edge scholarship in American Islam. Studies on the nature of religious violence are largely overlooked as well, despite a robust literature outlining the theoretical foundations of religious violence, including anthropological, sociological, and religious studies approaches.

TOWARD A BETTER UNDERSTANDING

Critical analysis of this book is indicative of the greater challenges to understanding Islam in prison. Perhaps the greatest obstacle for this work is its inability to account for other factors that contribute to inmate radicalization. Although the book is commendable for highlighting the role of prisons in the process, it oversimplifies complex tensions, including the and externally generated problems, the nature of post-release experiences, and the relationship between pre-prison and post-release experiences. Accounting for before-and-after prison experiences is critical for a fuller picture of radicalization.

At its core, the work takes a side in the longstanding debates among students of prison culture that pit importation theory against deprivation theory. It implicitly adopts a deprivation perspective, as indicated in statements like "radicalization emerges from personal strategies used by prisoners to cope with various conditions of their confinement." Although this is indeed true, a fuller understanding must also account for what inmates themselves import into the prison, including beliefs and attitudes. Taken to its logical extreme, the thesis suggests no need for concern at having the most hardened radicals all at the same institution—as long as they were kept in comfortable conditions of confinement.

A related difficulty for the text is the failure to recognize that many criminals, by definition, may be rightly seen as "radicals" in the first place. Although many are behind bars for relatively innocuous crimes, such as drug possession or property offenses, others are there for much more extreme behavior, including crimes of violence and involving the use of lethal weapons. These individuals have already demonstrated tendencies that veer from the norm toward the extremes, such as Kevin James. Hence to assert that such individuals were "radicalized" in prison misses the analytical mark and ignores that many behind bars are there as a result of behavior already deemed deviant.

The greatest existential threat thus has been and continues to be prison gangs, not the Muslim religion. The vilification of Islam ignores decades of prison outreach showing Muslim inmates actively using courts rather than violence to deal with grievances. Muslim prisoners have been at the forefront of the prisoner's rights movement and have litigated cases that have positively benefitted all prisoners, both expanding prisoners' rights and improving conditions of correctional facilities. Prison converts have also worked with the FBI to foil terrorist plots—something that gets no reference in the book. In the end, the book's framing of Muslim prisoners as terrorists amounts to just that—it is the framing of Muslim prisoners.

Conclusion

These chapters encapsulate an era of exploration into American punishment that provide a survey of contemporary prison culture, and particularly, the story of Islam behind bars. At a basic level they show it is absolutely necessary to consider the dynamics between prisons and religions to understand what is happening in the cultural present. For example, the turn to mass imprisonment may be read as a religious text in the same way chattel slavery can. More practically, there are consequences for society in such heavy reliance on imprisonment and the collateral consequences for prisoners and society.

While prisons might be characterized as public enemy number one for minority communities, they are also major hubs of Islamic conversion. In African-American culture, the prisoner-turned-Muslim is a famous trope, by now trite, which reveals a different side of prison facilities. Indeed, for many converts, prison is where they learned to straighten out their lives, shed past affiliations, and kneel before their God. With tens of thousands of individuals converting to Islam in prisons, the institutions continue to stand as an important feature of Islam in America. Collectively, prisons recruit individuals to the faith in numbers that dwarf the efforts of practically any Muslim group in the country. Their contribution to the American Muslim population is thus noteworthy, particularly when considering that for many of these individuals, the conversion is not some fad, but the beginning of a journey into Islam that evolves over time.

Whereas the value of religion in prison seems self-evident, there have been questions raised about radicalization as well. The available research has little to say about the process and few cases studies to illustrate the phenomenon. Instead, mere time spent in prison is often uncritically viewed as a catalyzing factor for violent radicalization. Such studies ignore an inmate's pre-prison experiences as well as those after release. More importantly, there is little causal evidence showing the imprisonment in some way caused radicalization. Thus, even though there is no doubt that prisons can become the source of oppression that creates radical inmates, whether this is occurring in American prisons to the level of terrorist recruitment seems less likely.

One might expect, with the sheer number of prisoners and popularity of Islam behind bars, we do not hear about more foiled or executed plots by prisoners who were radicalized in prison. With well over two million locked up in American jails and prisons, the notion of prison radical is a relatively short tale. Whereas individuals may become attracted to groups that are radical due to their racial orientations, this hardly means that violence is part of the plan. For those who convert to Islam, many embrace the religion as a path to peace, not terrorism. Hence, it is not coincidence that there has been little from the prisons by way of religious extremist violence.

Finally, this book hopes to have shown that there are ways to improve on the ongoing crises in criminal justice. There is much work to be done to make justice a reality for many. The legislature, judiciary, and executive branches could do so much more to reform the system. However, since, the brunt of criminal justice falls on poor and minority communities, those most culturally distant from affluent whites, the pace is at lag. Were the sons and daughters of judges, lawyers, and corporate America locked behind bars at the same rate, we would see a revolution. Until this happens, the American Bastille Day will indefinitely be put on pause. As such, this set of writings aims to agitate the status quo, to bring that Day around sooner rather than later.

APPENDIX

The chapters originally appeared in the publications below, which have links to the original version with full citations:

Chapter 1: RELIGION IN THE PRACTICE OF DAILY LIFE (Praeger, 2010), https://papers.ssrn.com/sol3/papers.cfm?abstract_id=1651139.

Chapter 2: RELIGION AND AMERICAN CULTURES: TRADITION, DIVERSITY AND POPULAR EXPRESSION (2nd ed.) (ABC-CLIO, 2015), https://papers.ssrn.com/sol3/papers.cfm?abstract_id=2551080.

Chapter 3: 82 MISS. L.J. 1 (2013), https://papers.ssrn.com/sol3/papers.cfm?abstract_id=2232897.

Chapter 4: --coauthored with Mary Rachel Gould, 33 SAINT LOUIS U. PUB. L. REV. 283 (2014), https://papers.ssrn.com/sol3/papers.cfm?abstract_id=2460531.

Chapter 5: 14 BERKELEY J. OF CRIM. L. 277 (2009), https://papers.ssrn.com/sol3/papers.cfm?abstract_id=1646652.

Chapter 6: 11 BERKELEY J. OF AFRICAN-AM. L. & POL'Y 84 (2009), https://papers.ssrn.com/sol3/papers.cfm?abstract_id=1647806.

Chapter 7: 37 WASH. U. J. L. & POL'Y. 89 (2011), https://papers.ssrn.com/sol3/papers.cfm?abstract_id=1966200.

Chapter 8: 37 SETON HALL L. REV. 497 (2007), https://papers.ssrn.com/sol3/papers.cfm?abstract_id=1646651.

Chapter 9: 22 BERKELEY LA RAZA L.J. 175 (2012), https://papers.ssrn.com/sol3/papers.cfm?abstract_id=1652121.

Chapter 10: 49 GONZAGA L. REV. 37 (2014), https://papers.ssrn.com/sol3/papers.cfm?abstract_id=2387928.

Chapter 11: 34 WHITTIER L. REV. 29 (2012), https://papers.ssrn.com/sol3/papers.cfm?abstract_id=2235706.

Chapter 12: 11 FL. INTL. U. L. REV. 201 (2015), https://papers.ssrn.com/sol3/papers.cfm?abstract_id=2767194.

Chapter 13: 90 CHICAGO-KENT L. REV. 495 (2015), https://papers.ssrn.com/sol3/papers.cfm?abstract_id=2572576.

Chapter 14: LATINOS AND CRIMINAL INJUSTICE (by Lupe Salinas, Michigan State U. Press, 2015), https://papers.ssrn.com/sol3/papers.cfm?abstract_id=2589112.

Chapter 15: INSTITUTE FOR SOCIAL POLICY & UNDERSTANDING (2013), https://papers.ssrn.com/sol3/papers.cfm?abstract_id=2206583.

Chapter 16: 39 T. MARSHALL L. REV. 225 (2014), https://papers.ssrn.com/sol3/papers.cfm?abstract_id=2488262.

CPSIA information can be obtained
at www.ICGtesting.com
Printed in the USA
FFOW04n1607160817
38776FF

9 781506 904870